Why Bother about the Poor?

The Politics of Poverty, Peace, and Development in Southern Africa

Yobert K. Shamapande

With Foreword by

The Anglican Archbishop of Cape Town

Njongonkulu W. H. Ndungane

who chaired a series of public hearings on
poverty eradication throughout South Africa

Bloomington, IN  Milton Keynes, UK

authorHOUSE®

AuthorHouse™
1663 Liberty Drive, Suite 200
Bloomington, IN 47403
www.authorhouse.com
Phone: 1-800-839-8640

AuthorHouse™ UK Ltd.
500 Avebury Boulevard
Central Milton Keynes, MK9 2BE
www.authorhouse.co.uk
Phone: 08001974150

First published by AuthorHouse 11/19/2007

ISBN: 978-1-4343-0742-2 (sc)

Library of Congress Control Number: 2007902886

Printed in the United States of America
Bloomington, Indiana

This book is printed on acid-free paper.

To Linah and our children —
my companions on the road!

TABLE OF CONTENTS

LIST OF TABLES

ABBREVIATIONS/ACRONYMS

ANC	African National Congress
BLS	Botswana, Lesotho and Swaziland
COSATU	Congress of South African Trade Unions
DRC	Democratic Republic of the Congo
DTA	Democratic Turnhalle Alliance
FAO	Food and Agriculture Organization of the United Nations
FNLA	National Front for the Liberation of Angola
FRELIMO	Front for the Liberation of Mozambique
ILO	International Labour Organization
IMF	International Monetary Fund
OAU	Organization of African Unity
MPLA	Popular Movement for the Liberation of Angola
NGO	Nongovernmental organization
RENAMO	Mozambique National Resistance
SACU	South African Customs Union
SADC	Southern Africa Development Community
SADCC	Southern African Development Coordination Conference

SAPs	structural adjustment programs
SWAPO	South West Africa People's Organization
TAZARA	Tanzania - Zambia Railway
UDF	United Democratic Front
UDI	Unilateral Declaration of Independence
UN	United Nations
UNDP	United Nations Development Programme
UNFPA	United Nations Population Fund
UNICEF	United Nations Children's Fund
UNIC	United Nations Information Centre
UNITA	National Union for the Total Independence of Angola
WHO	World Health Organization
ZANU-PF	Zimbabwe African National Union–Patriotic Front
ZAPU-PF	Zimbabwe African People's Union-Patriotic Front

FOREWORD

by The Anglican Archbishop of Cape Town,
The Most Reverend NJONGONKULU W. H. NDUNGANE

Eradication of poverty is a moral imperative. "They shall build houses; they shall plant vineyards," so the Scripture commands. And yet, societies have developed social walls that exclude the least fortunate amongst the inhabitants—women, children, the elderly, the disabled, and the destitute—the very people who should be at the center and beneficiaries of development programs.

Take our own country of South Africa. Although it is to be commended for its rapid embrace of the efforts to eliminate poverty, the reality remains bleak. Post-apartheid South Africa is a country with a highly developed infrastructure, industrialized economy, and pockets of urban affluence, but with millions of its people languishing in abject poverty, without access to constitutionally guaranteed basic services such as adequate housing, clean water, and health-care and employment opportunities. The educational system is almost chaotic with awfully inadequate facilities. The return of land to the dispossessed poor creeps along at a snail's pace.

We face monumental challenges in this region: military conflicts in Angola and the Democratic Republic of the Congo (DRC) rage on with devastating humanitarian consequences for the innocent civilian populations; floods have crippled Mozambique, rendering thousands of its people homeless and without livelihood; debt, HIV/AIDS, crime, violence, and unemployment ravage the region, causing untold misery and anguish. Everywhere poverty is on the increase, the quality of life diminishing, and life expectancy declining. We need to act swiftly to avert an impending catastrophe. We must reject the colonial and apartheid blind notion that somehow our people's poverty and suffering were *caused* by their poverty, the so-called "vicious circle of poverty" concept. People are poor today because yesterday they were victims, denied access to opportunities including essential services and, most critically, land. They were deprived of their basic human rights as well. People so long victimized by discrimination on all fronts and excluded from participatory decision-making in matters that affect their daily lives cannot suddenly develop.

There are vast political and strategic opportunities for the post-apartheid Southern Africa: we can now pursue a sustained, non-racial political harmony; wage war against poverty; promote social justice by removing glaring disparities in the distribution of income and wealth; and foster peaceful democratic transformation processes. As democratic institutions take on responsibilities of governance and grapple with the challenges of nation-building, they need to invest in the people. Combating poverty therefore requires a national commitment as a collective endeavor—a grand and active partnership by government, business, labor, non-governmental organizations (NGOs), including religious institutions, and, most importantly, the poor themselves. The poor must be at the forefront in the design and execution of projects intended to improve their well-being.

A central element in reducing poverty, I believe, is to develop a vision for society capable of creating a measure of national consensus—a consensus about equitable distribution of income, wealth, and assets. In other words, we need to formulate a "national project" with the eradication of poverty as its central thrust. I find this to be the basic inspiration that Dr. Shamapande's present work brings to this critical debate. How can social policy move the poverty-eradication agenda from words to concrete actions? He brilliantly lays bare the inherent contradictions and delineates some of the policy steps that must be taken to enable communities entrapped by conflict, poverty, and exclusion to work their way out of the crisis. By leveraging the capacities and creativity of the people, governments can reinforce peace and stability and provide the required inspiration for social upliftment.

Governments have an obligation to reduce poverty and bring about social relief, especially in rural areas, by investing directly in the people through provision of adequate basic requirements and social protections. They should not leave development to chance or settle for mere plans. Although plans have made elaborate provision of resources for rural projects, invariably most of those resources have found their way back to the affluent urban areas, consequently accentuating rural poverty and social cleavages.

In short, poverty eradication requires a firm political commitment in the allocation of resources to human-impact programs. As long as the vast majority of the population remains marginalized and the plight of the poor is not at the center of policy-making and national agenda, the region cannot succeed in becoming the land of opportunity that so many dreamed of and fought for.

Cape Town
South Africa
December 2000

PREFACE

The struggle for Southern Africa has been long and arduous. It began as a struggle against colonialism and imperialism, then became a resistance against apartheid South Africa and its occupation of Namibia, and culminated in a struggle against one-party dictatorship and statism that had overwhelmed Malawi and Zambia. Now, as a final chapter, Southern Africa must struggle for peace building and against abject poverty, inequalities, and social injustice that afflict millions of its inhabitants.

The purpose of this book is to critically review and contribute to the ongoing debate about the escalating poverty in the region, the policy implications and consequences for social progress. Three events triggered my writing it: first, it is the brainchild of two UN regional forums on poverty eradication in Southern Africa that we organized jointly as heads of United Nations Information Centres (UNICs) in South Africa, Namibia, and Zimbabwe. The forums were held in Windhoek, Namibia, and Midrand, South Africa, in May and November 1997, respectively. On behalf of my colleagues, I presented a paper on the theme of "why bother about the poor?" that generated much discussion and commentary. I argued in the presentation that it was the solemn responsibility of public policy to address and effectively mitigate the plight of the poor, the vulnerable, and the marginalized. The diversity of the presentations, participants, and results of those activities echoed that theme and brought into sharp focus the stark realities of extreme poverty, deprivation, and despair, especially among the rural people. Rural women, in particular, highlighted the life-and-death manifestations of poverty in their communities and of being subjected, on a daily basis, to 70–80 percent of unemployment and underemployment, as well as to chronic hunger, malnutrition, ill-health, alcoholism, infant mortality, and domestic violence. Public policy has, by and large, failed to decisively address their plight. This effort, therefore, is intended to take that debate forward in an attempt to define practical remedies to the problems that endanger so many lives on a daily basis.

Second, the nearly four years I served as UNIC director in South Africa were an extremely eventful period. In May 1996, the South African National Assembly adopted a new constitution that, for the first time, entrenched the basic human rights and fundamental freedoms of all its citizens. It turned out to be one of the most progressive constitutions ever adopted by any nation. In August 1997, South African civil society, supported by other partner organizations (including UN agencies resident in South Africa) gathered in Khayelitsha on the Cape Flats of Cape Town to declare war on poverty, proclaiming that "eradication of poverty … is a precondition to social justice, peace and security in our land. … We need a new moral order based on *ubuntu* that brings compassion and humanity into our homes and neighbourhoods." That effort was followed by a series of poverty hearings throughout the country chaired by Anglican Archbishop Njongonkulu Ndungane of Cape Town. Those hearings opened a window into the impoverished South Africa that eked out existence under heartrending conditions. The poverty hearings culminated in a civil society national poverty summit in Midrand, also chaired by Archbishop Ndungane. Subsequently, the South African government launched its own poverty and inequality study prepared under the auspices of the office of then deputy president Thabo Mbeki that further highlighted the legacies and utter social failure of the apartheid system to mitigate people's suffering. Meanwhile, the Truth and Reconciliation Commission hearings, chaired by Nobel laureate Archbishop Desmond Tutu, were grinding on and endlessly exposing the human rights horrors of the apartheid era. South Africans from all walks of life tried to come to terms and make peace with their tortured past.

Third, as a senior UN official, I became an active participant, deeply immersed in the tumultuous theater of militant activism that galvanized the civil society to confront the pressing issues of poverty, inequality, and social injustice among South Africans. Indeed, it could be argued that the real change in South Africa today is not that the once-oppressed victims of apartheid are suddenly better off, because they are not. The real change is symbolized by the heightened freedom to debate and dialogue at all levels of society about the critical issues of the time: poverty, inequalities, crime, race, and common welfare that have engendered intense passions.

My final reason for writing was more the result of a disappointment than motivation. In the course of our research on regional issues, my office in South Africa stumbled over a colorfully decorated study by the Southern African Development Community (SADC) Secretariat titled *1998 Official SADC Trade, Industry and Investment Reviews*. Not a word was said in that important document about any regional efforts to combat poverty and promote social investment. I was angry. Was that report written strictly to promote tourism and foreign investment, and was poverty not a subject important enough to warn policy makers and potential investors about? Extreme poverty was a stark reality in the region and could threaten tourism, investment, and even peace. To ignore or attempt to conceal it amounted to intellectual dishonesty that would undermine rather than enhance investor confidence. Investors and tourists would quickly realize the contradictions as they stepped off the plane, only to be greeted by food riots and rising crime waves on the streets of Harare, Johannesburg, and elsewhere. They may find themselves confronted with industrial and student unrest in the workplaces and on the campuses of higher learning. They could quickly notice the rapidly deteriorating and collapsing infrastructure, or they could find mass demonstrations by disgruntled peasants and unemployed veterans. All of these would dampen their drive to invest in our region. These things cannot be hidden. SADC should therefore be at the forefront of acknowledging its shortcomings, while at the same time highlighting its multifaceted strengths and the efforts being exerted to alleviate absolute poverty and bring about social upliftment in the region. These are endeavors to which serious investors would in fact want to render their support. I therefore decided it was time to make my voice heard by highlighting the compelling policy issues confronting the region.

I am in concrete on my thesis: just as the victims of unjust colonial and apartheid oppression rose to dismantle those systems, the poor of Southern Africa cannot be expected to remain passive forever in the face of mounting social injustice. They shall for sure rise up to reclaim their rights to human dignity. The potential danger to peace and democratic experiments posed by abject poverty should therefore not be underestimated. That danger was clearly demonstrated by the October 1997 attempted coup d'état in Zambia, by food riots in Zimbabwe, and by the endless conflicts over land in South Africa, Namibia, and Zimbabwe. We add to these the rising crime waves, labor unrests, and official corruption that continue to ravage the region and undermine its very economic viability. Thus, the promise of the twenty-first century being "Africa's century," of its renaissance, could turn out to be a pipe dream if it excludes the vast majority of the continent's people, those overwhelmed by the heavy weight of extreme poverty and social deprivation. Poverty in Southern Africa has the potential to re-ignite conflicts that would continue to thwart social progress on the same scale that the anti-colonial and anti-apartheid wars did for a generation.

I trust that this book will serve a useful purpose to expand the intellectual horizons, especially of young people, about the humanitarian crises facing our region. I shall also consider it to be successful if it can serve as a constant reminder that the real test of political leadership in our region lies not in the ability to win elections or ascend to power, but in the creative application of that power to enhance peace and tolerance among our people and to improve their human condition.

ACKNOWLEDGMENTS

This book has been a burden on me for six years now, and I am indebted for many things and to several people. I completed writing the book while I was on UN assignment in South Africa, and I am thankful to my loyal assistants, Mamodishe Sebati and Kgomotso Maditse, for their assistance in many ways. However, its publication, initially intended for 2001, was postponed twice. The first delay was caused by my transfer from South Africa back to UN Headquarters in New York to head the UN Development Business. While back in New York, I applied and tested many of the ideas and concepts contained in the book in teaching a course on the political economy of development in Southern Africa at Columbia University's School of International and Public Affairs during spring of 2000. Consequently, I revised portions of the work on the basis of intense interactions with students. I am grateful to my former students for their insightful inputs, and more especially to my colleagues, including Professor Coralie Bryant, Professor Stephen Cohen, and Dean Lisa Anderson for facilitating that assignment.

The second postponement was occasioned by my departure from the United Nations in December 2000 to run for president of Zambia. That, of course, turned out to be an overwhelming ordeal for the whole of 2001 without sparing a moment to look at the manuscript. For that exciting experience, I shall forever be indebted to colleagues in our party, the National Leadership for Development (NLD) for their confidence in nominating me and for the opportunity to contribute to the shaping of our national agenda. The courage, energy, and determination that many colleagues on the National Executive Committee and countless party officials at constituency and local levels brought to our campaign inspired thousands of our people, both young and old. We fought a good fight. And in the end, I am profoundly grateful to the Zambian people for believing in me and voting their conscience.

I am further indebted to the many 1997 UN regional forum participants in Namibia and South Africa, whose provocative presentations ignited the fire in me to write. I do hope the book captures some of the ideals, dreams, fears, experiences, and insights they conveyed with such powerful passions. In many ways, this is their book too and, hopefully, it will reach as many of them in the region as possible. With so many of them, along with my good friend and colleague Finjap Njinga, then UNIC Director in Namibia, we argued into the late hours of the night over some of the ideas and concepts captured in this volume. However, I do take full responsibility for documenting them here, and hopefully with a good degree of accuracy. Obviously, as it should be, I have also extensively injected into this work my own views and convictions. My sincere appreciation also goes to Leonora Khanyile for taking time out from her very busy activities of NGOs in Johannesburg to chair the regional poverty forum held in South Africa. To Anglican Archbishop Njongonkulu Ndungane, I shall forever be grateful for his generosity in inviting me to the poverty hearings that he chaired throughout South Africa, and for agreeing to write a foreword to this book. He is a towering inspiration in our region for the broader quest for social justice. I am further thankful to a dear friend and former UN colleague, Dr. Wilfred Asombang, for painstakingly reading the entire manuscript and offering useful comments and suggestions. To Dr. Joseph Diescho, words escape me to express my gratitude to that fellow for his help on the book and, more especially, for his long personal and intellectual friendship spanning more than two decades since the 1980s when we toiled together in the trenches of the Namibian struggle for independence. Thanks Joe, for being there and for constantly staying in touch during those rough-and-tumble days of my 2001 presidential campaign in Zambia.

Finally, I owe my deepest debt of gratitude to the real pillars of my life: my wife, Linah, for being that special person and a towering power of strength, and our children. They have had to redefine patience and sacrifice by staying with me during the many trying moments and tolerating my constant interruptions of our quality time together for me to complete this project.

Yobert K. Shamapande
Lusaka, Zambia
May 2004

PROLOGUE:

WHY I RAN FOR PRESIDENT OF ZAMBIA IN 2001

Finally, on the morning of December 28, 2001, the Zambian elections were behind us. The Zambian people had spoken. We lost but were not defeated. Some may ask if the effort was worth it. Absolutely! I believe it was. I left the United Nations in December 2000 to run for president of Zambia because I wanted to make a difference in the lives of ordinary Zambians—to offer the committed leadership the country so desperately needed to improve the human condition. That dream, that ideal, that vision, and that journey shall live on.

More appropriately, the answer to the above question must be found in what was at stake in 2001. When I entered the presidential race, Zambia was on its knees: wrecked by an 80 to 90 percent extreme poverty rate that afflicted unspeakable social misery; 60 percent unemployment; severe hunger that left more than 50 percent of the country's children malnourished and with stunted growth; collapsed education and dysfunctional health-care services; escalating illiteracy levels and ill-health; one million street children; HIV/AIDS pandemic that ravaged one in every five Zambians; lack of social protections for the poor and especially the most vulnerable elderly, retirees, women,

1

children, and rural people; and, above all, widespread corruption and graft that left a real sense of despair and hopelessness among the people. And there was a total collapse in the country's social delivery system. Thus Zambia's very survival or preservation was at stake. That was after ten years of the Movement for Multiparty Democracy (MMD) in government, and before that, twenty-seven years of United National Independence Party (UNIP) rule. To say that both of them had failed the Zambian people would be an understatement. And, surprisingly, both MMD and UNIP were vying hard to return to power in 2001 to inflict five more years of their destructive policies. Obviously, the Zambian people had now had enough of politics as usual. They wanted change, real change that would bring about an immediate impact on their daily lives, not just the promises or empty political slogans they had been fed for more than three decades. But ordinary Zambians, meanwhile, lacked the voice with which to mitigate the critical issues of the day or to challenge the power structures in the society.

By any standards, the kind of social crises besetting Zambia at that point represented a national disaster, an emergency of major proportions requiring an emergency response. But, unfortunately, the ruling elites of Zambia saw it differently; they were unmoved. They failed to reorder national priorities to tackle effectively the pressing challenges of the day. They continued to tinker around the development margins. That, in no small measure, forced many ordinary Zambians, including myself, to get involved in the country's political process. It was time to fundamentally change the direction of our country. There could be no nobler cause than the struggle to save human lives, preserve society, and promote social justice. That's what was at stake in 2001, and therefore the struggle was not in vain.

In that year, it also became clear that Zambians were looking for a different brand of national leadership; they wanted a leadership with *clean hands*, people not involved in the looting of national wealth that led to the impoverishment of the country. They wanted *qualified* and *committed* leadership, people with background, experience, exposure, and vision to truly change the country for the better. And, more importantly, they wanted leadership with a *plan,* an *action program* capable of addressing their daily plight and wrenching them from abject poverty, hunger, unemployment, illiteracy, ill-health, and the devastating impact of HIV/AIDS that had ravaged the society. They wanted leadership to address the moral crises facing the country, including the phenomenon of street children and lack of social protections for the most vulnerable such as women, children, the elderly, retirees, unemployed, homeless, orphans; the list was endless. In short, Zambians were crying out for a new, visionary leadership with fresh ideas and an abiding dedication to improving their standard of living and quality of life. They were in no mood to recycle the same tired politicians who had so miserably failed them in the past.

The Calling of Public Service

Public service or politics, in my view, is the virtue to fight for a cause. That also demands individual sacrifice and the ability to stand fast for principle, for an ideal, at risk to oneself, one's future, or indeed the well-being of one's family. To venture into politics for less than those ideals amounts to a betrayal of oneself and of the electorate one seeks to serve. That cause, that principle, and that ideal, for me, has been and will always be the pursuit of social justice—the pursuit to improve the welfare of the powerless in society, those whose voices have been silenced, rights violated, or opportunities denied.

But first things first. I was born to peasant parents on November 30, 1941 (or so my older brother told me as no birth certificates were issued in colonial days especially to black children born in rural areas) in Chief Mungule's area of Kabwe rural (now Chibombo) district in the Central Province of Zambia. My father, Mwaliwanika Shamapande Kananga and blind mother, Chilimba Mulimo, were smallholder farmers with no education and of only limited means. I was thus raised and cultured in the harsh environment of rural Zambia, and the values I hold emanate from that humble upbringing. I have an abiding appreciation for rural areas and life. As a child of a blind mother, I was told that odds were very much stacked against me. By all accounts, I could have died in infancy, either through accidental injury or from some other mishap. But I survived, largely due to the collective diligence of my siblings and extended family. My survival also demonstrated that despite the odds and deprivation associated with family disabilities, rural living, and lack of social protections, a collectivity of the poor themselves can make a difference in life-and-death situations.

Educationally, I was equally handicapped in a number of ways. As a rural child, I had no access to early childhood education until I started primary school at Muchenje (Seventh Day Adventist) and Kapopo (Catholic) schools. Second, the long distances we had to traverse to get to the nearest school made education almost physically inaccessible in rural areas at that time. As a result, I started school late—around the age of eight or nine—when I was sufficiently mature to make the long distances to and from school alone. However, I subsequently moved to Matero (Catholic) primary school in Lusaka, where I completed primary education. From there, I proceeded to St. Paul's (Catholic) secondary school, Mulungushi in Kabwe, and later to Chizongwe (public) secondary school in Chipata, where I completed secondary school education.

The arrival of Zambia's political independence in 1964 brought enormous opportunities, especially for the young people. It was followed by the most productive ten-year period in the country's educational enterprise. It opened up opportunities in terms of formal or informal education, vocational training, skills development, and higher learning in Zambia. Virtually every school in the country became a life-long learning center day and night. Opportunities included the promotion of adult literacy programs, expanded primary and secondary education, including postsecondary or college training, leading to the establishment of the University of Zambia in 1966. Independence also released unsurpassed energies for the youth and students of Zambia to get involved more intensely in the country's political and development debate of the day.

Throughout my school years, I was an ardent student activist and advocate of student rights and inclusion. While at Chizongwe in 1964, I started my first direct involvement in student politics and governance following my election as provincial secretary of the National Union of Northern Rhodesian (later Zambian) Students. Also elected along with me to our Eastern Province Executive Committee were the late William Kayamba as president, the late Zakeyo Zimba as publicity secretary, and Potpher Kabandami as chairman, among others. In my capacity, I advocated for a strong student voice and involvement in school administration. That brought me into conflict with then school principal John Nelson, who in 1965 had succeeded a retiring more seasoned educationist and administrator, Alfred King. John Nelson was contemptuous of independence and a black African government. He viewed any student involvement in politics as a waste of time and an unwarranted diversion from academics. He thus sought to muzzle the student voice as much as possible in perpetuation of colonial policies. I wrote a scathing editorial in the student newsletter challenging his "colonial mentality" in school administration and urging direct government intervention to ensure a fair treatment of students. As a result, I and seven other colleagues were suspended from school, but we were subsequently reinstated following direct government intervention.[1]

Immense intellectual grounding, discovery, and growth characterized my educational journey in America during the 1960s and 1970s while studying in California and New York. That period also coincided with some of the most eventful years in American history. Colleges and universities became hotbeds of social and student activism, characterized by profound transformation and rethinking of the various underlying paradigms of human development. Civil rights movements were grinding on, and the country's poor agitated for a stronger voice in society. Campaigns for civil rights, social justice, and against the Vietnam War resonated and gained momentum in the urban neighborhoods, streets, and especially on college campuses. The tipping point was reached when riots erupted in several communities of Los Angeles, Chicago, Newark, and other cities. These were followed by the assassinations of Reverend Dr. Martin Luther King Jr. in April 1968 and of New York Senator Robert F. Kennedy in June of the same year. Meanwhile, the American youths nationwide questioned the moral efficacy of continued military adventurism in Vietnam and elsewhere and rebelled against military draft and service. In response to the growing unrest, the Lyndon Johnson administration, among other things, launched the "Great Society" initiatives and the war on poverty to address some of the sources of social discontent; new civil and voting rights laws were passed, opening doors to education, housing, and democratic participation for the hitherto excluded black Americans; and in 1969, America's scientific and technological advances opened new human frontiers by landing a man on the moon.

In the academia, social scientists, development economists, philosophers, historians, as well as activists from every continent began to vigorously question the conventional wisdom of the development thought and to espouse new theories about the meaning of social progress. The purely capitalist mode of production that emphasized growth to the exclusion of equitable distribution of wealth and poverty reduction came under severe attack. Instead, there was an emerging social thought of a people-centered development or development with a human face guided by the principle of interventionist public policy. Those theorists also offered penetrating analyses of the structures of human poverty, basic social needs, and the policy interventions required to improve standards of living and the quality of human life, especially in developing nations. In the end, even the World Bank, an ardent bastion of the capitalist model firmly anchored ideologically in growth alone, joined the new chorus embracing growth with redistribution. Collectively, therefore, my generation came to internalize the imperatives of development as a people-centered program intended to reduce and eradicate human poverty and promote social equity. In short, we came to believe in the principle that the primary goal or end product of development was to improve the human condition—to endow people with greater economic choices, greater opportunities, and possibilities toward greater social progress.

My professional engagements further served to profoundly reinforce my educational experiences. As a town planner for the City of Lusaka, I derived a deeper fulfillment, not from the grand design of the Greater Lusaka Master Plan but from how well we managed the social deliverables in the site and service schemes and squatter upgrading program. We actually put roofs on people's heads, brought roads and sanitation and clean water to their doorsteps. In more than two decades with the United Nations, I was confronted with the pressing question of Namibian decolonization and the higher moral issues of human rights, freedoms, and delivery of humanitarian assistance to the oppressed and underprivileged refugee populations including women, children, and the disabled. Working with Martti Ahtisaari of Finland and subsequent UN commissioners for Namibia, leadership of the South West Africa People's Organization (SWAPO) and governments of Southern Africa, we developed strategies for the political and economic decolonization of Namibia and post-conflict rebuilding of the country and the region. More profoundly, the Namibian struggle taught me the imperatives of providing timely basic, life-sustaining humanitarian requirements on a massive scale—food, shelter, water, medicines—to the suffering refugees living in squalid conditions in Angola, Botswana, Zambia, Zimbabwe, and elsewhere. Sadly, at that time our efforts could only alleviate human suffering among Namibians but not eradicate poverty or bring development or indeed social justice. Only free Namibians themselves, living in a free country, could achieve those higher attributes of nation-building.

Following the demise of apartheid in South Africa, UN Secretary-General Boutros Boutros-Ghali assigned me to South Africa to, among other mandates, add the UN's voice to South Africa's reintegration into the international community while, at the same time, supporting its internal post-apartheid transformation. In collaboration with the South African government, civil society organizations, and various stakeholders, we addressed the critical issues concerning the legacies of apartheid including extreme poverty, social and income inequalities, massive unemployment, human and gender rights, discrimination, as well as the compelling crises imposed by the growing numbers of people infected with HIV/AIDS, drug abusers, orphans, and the homeless.

Clearly, those were some of the powerful human events and influences that profoundly impacted my life and sense of conviction. They shaped my political perspectives about the critical issues of human development, poverty, social equity, and the meaning of fundamental justice.

OPPONENTS AND DIVERGENT VISIONS

Elections are about choices and about the debate to define a new national agenda. I entered the 2001 presidential race to contribute to the expansion of those choices and the reshaping of Zambia's development agenda. The results of those elections were unique in that there was no real winner but only big losers—the Zambian people. The so-called MMD "winner" actually lost the elections given the fact that he secured only 29 percent of the total vote as compared with the combined 71 percent received by the "losing" opposition. The 71 percent of the Zambian voters, who queued up for endless hours in the sweltering heat determined to bring about a meaningful change, were in the end the greatest losers in those flawed elections. They did not see the fruits of their labor. They felt cheated and badly betrayed! But more critically, they have had to endure five more years of the same failed leadership of the past decades.

Be that as it may, democracy won in 2001. We were eleven presidential candidates: Gwendoline Konie of the Social Democratic Party (SDP), Tilyenji Kaunda of UNIP, Anderson Mazoka of the United Party for National Development (UPND), Brigadier General Godfrey Miyanda of the Heritage Party (HP), Michael Sata of the Patriotic Front (PF), Pastor Nevers Mumba of the National Citizens Coalition (NCC), Benjamin Mwila of the Zambia Republican Party (ZRP), Levy Mwanawasa of the ruling MMD, Dr. Inonge Mbikusita-Lewanika of the Agenda for Zambia (AZ), Lieutenant General Christon Tembo of the Forum for Democracy and Development (FDD), and myself standing on the NLD ticket. We presented stark choices, energized democracy, and gave multiparty pluralism a real meaning in Zambia. We crisscrossed the country and took our message directly to the Zambian people. To say that the 2001 presidential elections in Zambia were an earth-shaking event would be an understatement. And, in my view, that momentous event will probably not recur in the foreseeable future.

It would be presumptuous of me to attempt an assessment of the driving motives for running or the caliber of each of my esteemed opponents. Suffice it to say that, with the exception of two or three, all candidates had what it took to seek the presidency of Zambia at that stage in time: we all had formal education or some professional qualification; we had track records of performance, of having run something in our professional careers; and, more importantly, we had made serious pledges and commitments, if elected, to improve the human condition, the material well-being of our fellow Zambians.

But that was just about where our similarities ended. Our visions and philosophical divergences were deep and profound. They were largely shaped by the knowledge, experiences, exposures, and perspectives we brought to the campaign. Many of the candidates represented more of the same, and only a few of us were truly new in the political arena and came to the table with fresh ideas. Five of those opponents (Tembo, Miyanda, Mwanawasa, Sata, and Mwila) had served in the high echelons of the previous MMD government, under which Tembo, Miyanda, and Mwanawasa also held the position of vice president of both government and party. With the exception of Mwanawasa, who resigned the vice presidency in protest in 1994, all the others were dismissed from MMD before forming their own separate organizations. The internal differences leading to their dismissal from MMD were as a result of former president Frederick Chiluba's third-term bid and his subsequent nomination of Mwanawasa, who others regarded as an outsider, to become the MMD presidential candidate. Clearly they did not leave on account of principle or any philosophical differences over MMD's destructive polices. Thus the MMD party as a whole had a lot to account for in the 2001 elections. As a result, those former government officials, while admitting that the country was in dire economic straits, campaigned on the same failed MMD policies as the new remedies for the country—they advocated the same tinkering around the economic margins in the hope of achieving different results. Basically, they campaigned on the premise that recycling the same old wine in new bottles would somehow improve its taste. Not so. And the Zambian people were fully conscious of that folly this time around. Better application of the same failed methods would not do the trick of improving the people's standards of living or quality of life. Obviously that group of former MMD leaders placed a heavy premium on their government experience as the necessary qualification for the election to the leadership of the country, without which, they thought, one would be engaged in "on-the-job training." Ironically, when pressed to explain why MMD, which they served for ten years, had performed so abysmally, they quickly distanced themselves from those policies and disowned any collective responsibility of governance. The critical issue here for the country was not the errors committed by an individual leader—Chiluba—but the failure of the MMD policies as a whole.

Zambians today have become increasingly impatient. They are in a real hurry to improve their social condition. It would be naïve and absolutely unjustifiable for any Zambian government to adopt a gradualist approach to addressing the country's extreme social misery. It would certainly be unforgivable to repeat the same destructive policies of the previous regimes. The country has remained on its knees today because yesterday the leadership of both UNIP and MMD failed to establish a firm foundation for development. While UNIP started off well and achieved some positive results soon after independence, it lost direction on the way in pursuit of amassing political power through the introduction of a one-party state. The MMD leadership, on the other hand, squandered the people's goodwill from the start as it pursued the destructive policies and practices of personal wealth accumulation to the detriment of all national development.

Thus, on the development front, UNIP had absolutely nothing to offer in 2001 that it failed to achieve in its twenty-seven years in power. On the same score, MMD had nothing new to offer to the people of Zambia in 2001 that it failed to do in its ten-year period of misrule. It had had ten years to make a difference, a decade of undivided goodwill and anticipation of the Zambian people, but it was all squandered. Instead, MMD presided over the destructive policies leading to the deep impoverishment of the country and its people. By the same token, those MMD offshoots including HP, FDD, SDP, ZRP, and PF were equally impotent as they were part and parcel of the MMD's failed policies and ten-year misrule. The former MMD leaders who headed new parties could not claim innocence because they were collectively the principal architects who designed, implemented, and defended the programs that brought about untold human misery among Zambians. They therefore did not espouse any new ideas in 2001, and, if elected, they could not possibly have performed any differently from their parent MMD.

What was clear, however, was that those former MMD leaders were people with abundant resource endowment and unlimited means who, having served close to the presidency, believed that it was their turn to lead. But those were hardly the compelling justifications for seeking leadership at such a critical time in the country's history, when Zambia was bleeding and needed rescue. What further baffled me was the unabashed opportunism displayed by AZ and NCC in those elections. While professing to pursue independent programs, it turns out that both AZ and NCC were apparently appendages of MMD. What did the leaders of those parties really stand for if at the drop of a hat they could abandon principles, dissolve their parties, and join MMD soon after the elections? Inonge Mbikusita-Lewanika was the first to dissolve AZ to join MMD, and she was appointed as Zambia's ambassador to Washington. Subsequently, Nevers Mumba dribbled his fellow opposition leaders, who had counted on him as their spokesman, to accept the prize as the vice president to Mwanawasa, only to be dismissed from that post nine months later. Their actions served to lend credence to what I had all along dismissed as a falsehood that MMD had sponsored certain small parties for the purpose of fragmenting the opposition. Ironically, prior to elections, both AZ and NCC were at the forefront in calling for the formation of the so-called "government of national unity" among the opposition parties to oust MMD from power. Thus, I would argue that theirs was an equally empty stand in those elections. Therefore, the only two genuine political parties to engage in an honest debate about fresh ideas and new policies to address Zambia's mounting social plight were Mazoka's UPND and our NLD, although obviously distinctions existed in our policy strategies and prescriptions.

However, because UPND had a head start, it had designed a sound national program and assembled an impressive array of required manpower to deliver. The party had been on the ground and running for some three years. It also represented a real choice, and but for the unfortunate election manipulations, I believe UPND actually won the presidency in 2001, and I said so at the time. In addition, that party had the capacity to pursue meaningful reforms intended to bring about economic improvement and social progress in Zambia.

As for NLD, we waged a focused and principled campaign grounded in the conviction that Zambia was ravaged by extreme poverty, suffering, and pain, conditions that called for taking immediate and equally extreme remedial measures. Regrettably, we were on the ground for only six months before elections. We espoused a vision of fresh ideas, social reforms, and, more critically, of a radical reordering of national priorities including the launch of an emergency recovery program to bring about immediate social relief within the first one hundred days of our taking office. NLD, therefore, tabled a bold and ambitious national agenda intended to (a) combat abject poverty and bring about immediate social relief through a massive public works job creation and opportunities expansion program, (b) subsidize agriculture and guarantee national food security for every Zambian household, (c) put all one million street children into schools and provide them with appropriate care, (d) fight the HIV/AIDS pandemic through prevention, access to affordable antiretroviral drugs, and proper care for the victims including orphans, (e) support workers' rights by rolling back laws and legislation hostile to labor and preserve the principles of one industry, one union, (f) adjust retirees' pensions to reflect the cost-of-living conditions as a result of the constant devaluation of the kwacha, (g) abolish the value added tax (VAT), streamline the tax structure by making it more progressive, pro-poor and pro-low income groups, and (h) launch a national social protection scheme to address the plight of the most vulnerable in our society including the disabled, elderly, retirees, rural women, children, and the unemployed.

To turn the country around, we advocated for a social compact with the Zambian people to be accomplished through tackling targeted tasks within specified time frames. First, Zambia needed firm proactive measures to put people to work again through a national public works effort, accompanied by vigorous reindustrialization measures to generate growth and create employment opportunities with living wages. Our campaign swings on the Copperbelt revealed a truly painful picture of a staggering industrial devastation and mass unemployment. Dunlop of Ndola, once the giant tire producer, was gone, with tires now being imported from South Africa. Chloride, Supa Loaf, Zambia Steel, and other industrial outlets that once stood as symbols of Copperbelt's industrial prowess were scrapped. Meanwhile, the demise of mines threw tens of thousands of workers out of jobs, condemning Luanshya, Kalulushi, Kantanshi, and many other cities into looking like ghost towns.

Second, we believed that the country needed to place immediately, or within one hundred days, all one million street children into schools and provide them with proper care. This was an inescapable national emergency and security obligation requiring an emergency response. It would be supported by a declaration of a universal, compulsory, and free public education until grade twelve. Grade twelve was chosen because that was the stage at which youngsters attained reasonable maturity for employment. Meanwhile, fee-paying private schools would, of course, continue to be encouraged as a means of expanding educational opportunities and choices for the people.

Third, Zambians needed a vigorous program to alleviate, reduce, and eradicate poverty and create a poverty-free, hunger-free, peaceful, and prosperous society in preparation for attaining the established global standards by the year 2015. To achieve that would entail a radical reordering of national priorities and setting of goals, targets, and timetables that were entirely deliverable, expanded poverty-reduction measures firmly anchored in guaranteeing social safety nets to the poor and the most vulnerable, and in the delivery of affordable services for the people.

Fourth, we urgently needed a program to rebuild the country's social infrastructure including first-rate education and first-class health-care services that were once readily accessible and responsive to the people's needs and ability to pay.

Fifth, we proposed a social compact for Zambia to provide hunger relief and guarantee food security for every household in the country on a sustainable long-term basis. Rural Zambia would again be the bastion of food production and agricultural activity that it once was so as to ensure that no child would again fall victim to malnourishment, hunger, or stunted growth.

Sixth, we advocated for a social covenant to promote active youth participation and gender equality in national governance, to utilize the talents and skills of the two largely marginalized social groups in the country. Real modern human development and national rebuilding to take root in Zambia would require an inclusive society that integrated women and youth in the development agenda.

Finally, we argued that Zambia needed a more proactive program to fight the devastating impact of the HIV/AIDS pandemic through prevention, access to affordable medicines including antiretroviral drugs, and expansion of facilities to care for the victims including orphans.

These were not empty political slogans. To NLD, they constituted a binding contract with the Zambian people, an enduring commitment to lifting the heavy burden of abject poverty and social deprivation that had pinned them down for so long. We were on a real mission to confront the pressing challenges facing the country and, in the words of the slain African American civil rights leader Martin Luther King Jr., "to hew a tunnel of hope through a mountain of despair." Thus, our message of hope resonated.

The intense political activism brought about by the 2001 elections resulted in the opposition parties collectively winning the presidential elections with 71 percent of the total vote, although they lost the presidency to the ruling MMD's Mwanawasa, who received only 29 percent of the votes. That fundamental electoral contradiction was primarily precipitated by the flawed national constitution and encouraged by a compromised Electoral Commission of Zambia (ECZ) that organized the elections.

That is why I rejected as contemptible nonsense the suggestion that the opposition lost the presidential race because we had split the votes or were somehow disorganized. Those were obviously the views of casual observers. Had there been a run-off election, one of the opposition candidates would have triumphed outright. Here, too, were some of the real, incontrovertible benefits of those elections that must be acknowledged. We changed the political landscape of Zambia, forever I believe. Elections are about choices, choices of competing ideologies and of contesting ideas. For the first time in Zambia's history, the electorate was able to choose from eleven presidential candidates and their starkly competing philosophies and visions about the future of our country. Also for the first time in the country's history, we had two female candidates aspiring for the highest office in the land. Clearly, we also broke the cycle of a one-party monopoly in Zambia, for good I hope. For the first time ever, we had a truly democratic, multiparty elected parliament to give the Zambian people a stronger voice. And for the first time, the city halls of our country, including those of the capital city of Lusaka and other municipal and rural councils, became truly multiparty democratic institutions, not directly controlled as the tools of the ruling party. Our people began to enjoy and exercise their constitutionally guaranteed freedoms of expression and association. As a result, the mayor of Lusaka could, for the first time, claim to be too preoccupied with the business of city governance instead of dashing off to the airport to parade dutifully whenever the president was leaving for or returning from foreign trips. And last, our competing visions and philosophies also resonated throughout the land and empowered people. We inspired the young and old alike to dream of greater heights and to demand of themselves and their government greater deeds. Zambians today know that a government is best that serves as their servant and not their master. They now expect their government that professes to be truly caring to also deliver.

Personally, I came away from those elections with a sense of great satisfaction with the fact that we raised the standards of political discourse in the country, that we gave a voice and hope to the voiceless and those in despair, and that the rich agenda we espoused contributed significantly to enhancing democracy. If these efforts represented disorganization, then, as I trust most Zambians do, I prefer a chaotic democratic pluralism enriched with a vibrant public debate to an orderly and passive one-party dictatorship.

But was I disappointed? Of course I had my own disappointments about those elections. Foremost among them was the fact that we lost because of my inability to convince those wavering voters that I was not late in arriving on the political scene. I was not late because our party was launched in May 2001, whereas the MMD offshoots of PF, HP, and FDD came much later in the year. But no one ever questioned their timing. Apparently those who argued that I was late actually meant to say that I was an unknown political figure, having not served in senior capacities in the previous government administrations whose policies had brought much destruction to the country. Obviously, if that was one of the qualifications, then I did not need it and made no apologies for that. My background and qualifications, educationally and professionally, spoke volumes. I did not need the imprimatur of failed regimes. I was the only candidate in the race with tested development management knowledge and experience and the ability to articulate the real issues about getting Zambia out of its economic quagmire without shrouding my message in the usual wishy-washy political chicanery. I meant what I said and said what I meant! Moreover, my work with the Lusaka City Council, the depth of my UN experiences in the decolonization of Namibia and development of a blueprint for post-independence reconstruction of that country, my role in drawing up UN assistance programs to the frontline states in the aftermath of apartheid South Africa's destabilization of the region, and my stint in the post-apartheid transformation efforts of South Africa were incontestable. Therefore I was convinced that it was time for me to bring those skills, experiences, and perspectives to bear on the improvement of the Zambian condition. Further, I had an unshakable confidence and faith in the Zambian people's sense of fundamental fairness. Zambians understood their mission well in those elections and responded accordingly. They could not, at that stage in the country's history, elect the same politicians who were responsible for the unspeakable destruction of their country. That's why they voted overwhelmingly for the opposition.

My profound disappointment was with the extremely poor conduct of the elections by ECZ. It was a sad commentary that, after nearly forty years of independence, Zambia still had a less-than-professional electoral commission to organize and supervise a credible national election process before, during, and after the vote. The registration of voters was a logistical nightmare; some voters did not know where to register, and those who knew were subjected to endless, ever-shifting, and unreasonable deadlines. One could not help but wonder whether the ECZ's goal was to curtail rather than expand the people's democratic participation. During the campaign period, the presidential debates, though vibrant, were stifled by the constant maneuvering and by the ruling MMD and the non-participation of its candidate, who had much to defend about the disastrous policies of his party. And sadly, at every stage in determining the ground rules for those debates, the ECZ decided in favor of the MMD, whose well-known strategy was to minimize the exposure to the national audience of its candidate for fear of unmasking the party's unpopular image. The MMD even went to the extent of blocking the final presidential debate scheduled for the evening before the vote in defiance of a high court injunction authorizing that debate to go forward. Obviously, the MMD must have known that structures were in place for its candidate to triumph in the elections regardless of lack of exposure to the voters. Those debates were, in my judgment, critical job interviews with the Zambian people, and, in my profession, any candidate who failed to attend an interview never got the job! On voting day, the situation was equally chaotic as the ECZ lacked the capacity, manpower, and mobility to deliver voting materials on time and to supervise a credible election. The opening and closing of polls was sporadic and erratic; the ECZ's capacity to detect irregularities, corruption, vote-buying, and so on, and to protect the integrity of the election was nonexistent. Vote counting was equally chaotic, as it was done selectively instead of systematically. The ECZ reporting of the results conveyed the perception that it was intended to influence the polling patterns in favor of the ruling-party candidate in those centers where voting was still in progress. Indeed, rumor had it that some votes first went to the State House for counting before going to the Mulungushi Conference Election Center for reporting.

I was further disappointed and frustrated that the importance of issues and ideas in those elections was terribly diminished by the presence of too much money, leading to allegations of massive vote buying, bribery, and other violations. Corruption irregularities were rampant and particularly damaging in an environment hard hit by extreme poverty, making voters highly susceptible to manipulation. Democracy itself was defeated the moment people began to buy or sell votes. More critically, political parties like the NLD, whose strength rested in the debate of ideas and not in dishing out money, became severely disadvantaged. In that respect as well, the ECZ let down the Zambian people and failed to protect the integrity of the vote. The election was thus inherently neither free nor fair.

The other regret I had related to the biased media reporting of the elections, in particular by the state-run Zambia National Broadcasting Corporation television, radio, and newspaper services. The so-called public broadcaster became entirely a propaganda machine for the ruling MMD. Its candidate was allowed to monopolize access to the public media, while only scanty, paid-for coverage was given to his ten opponents. Moreover, even the so-called independent media were equally selective in their coverage in favor of relations, aunties, uncles, or friends involved in the race, instead of being issue driven as is the common practice in more mature democracies.

Last, I was deeply troubled by the controversies surrounding the final outcome of the elections. Massive rigging, pure and simple, seemed to characterize the elections and therefore the results! Election manipulations invariably had the effect of dampening the people's enthusiasm for democracy because they were denied the right to reap the fruits of their labor. All reputable election observers, including those from the European Union, the American-based Carter Center, the local Coalition 2001, and the Foundation for a Democratic Process, were emphatic that the elections were flawed, that they did not reflect the will of the Zambian people. That also explained why there were so many protests on the streets of Zambia and in parliament, as well as election petitions that flooded our courts. The only observer groups that reached different conclusions were the SADC Parliamentary Forum and OAU, notorious, in similar situations, of routinely endorsing the party in power. Obviously the flawed conduct of the 2001 elections left a sad imprint on Zambia's otherwise noble efforts to enrich democracy. The country still has a long road to traverse if it is to reclaim and eventually nurture the underlying values of a democratic dispensation.

Where Do We Go From Here?—
"Melting Pot" or Chaos

Zambia still has a mountain of a job to climb. After the 2001 elections, the country has not yet healed. Poverty is confronting; it is a sorry sight of a massive human tragedy brought about by failed policies. Meanwhile, political confrontations have deepened. The disputed presidential election remains before the courts, thus debilitating the incumbent president's performance. The task force investigating the plunder of national resources by the previous regime is grinding on, leading to the indictment on multiple offences of former president Frederick Chiluba and several of his former lieutenants. Presidential appointments of opposition members of parliament to executive government posts exacerbated rather than healed existing cleavages. The establishment of a Constitutional Review Commission has also backfired, as civil society has called it a bluff and vowed to mobilize against its findings. Even the recent appointment of Pastor Nevers Mumba to the vice presidency, a move intended to pacify the opposition, has proved to be divisive, as the man not only lacked credible qualifications but performed more like an MMD cadre; he was unceremoniously dropped after nine months in office. And to the surprise of many, both government and opposition leaders are criss-crossing the country, holding campaign rallies to promote meaningless programs or to explain largely useless and unjustifiable policies. In the meantime, however, development has retarded and people's suffering continued.

Clearly, Zambia's future now must confront three underlying scenarios: the country's development could either stagnate for a long time; or it could retrogress into even greater chaos than at the moment; or, through some judicious application of its vast resource potential, Zambia could recover and achieve considerable social progress. These are the daunting challenges the country faces. Each of these options, however, would be driven by a set of policy determinants. Under the first scenario, stagnation would come about as a result of the current policies of missed opportunities and misdirected priorities. The present priority appears to be only the rooting out of public corruption and recovery of plundered national assets. While these are entirely commendable goals, Zambia needs to do more to bring about social relief that people so desperately need. There must be proactive initiatives to promote recovery and social development without which there would be no progress. That was what the 2001 elections were all about. The country cries out for a coherent recovery program to reduce extreme poverty, rebuild education and health-care services, create employment opportunities, fight the HIV/AIDS pandemic, combat hunger and guarantee food security for all, afford street children education and proper care, and protect the most needy of our fellow citizens. These efforts would of course demand massive resource investment in funds and skills and, above all, committed leadership to ensure policy delivery. But we all recognize the fact that the current Mwanawasa administration lacks the manpower skills required for effective national program delivery. Skills are dispersed among the various political parties and Zambian professionals who have drifted abroad in search of greener pastures. Therefore, if the MMD persists in going it alone and the current status quo remains, Zambia's development will certainly falter and stagnate. The people's hardships and suffering will remain a way of life.

As for the second scenario, the potential exists for the country to degenerate into even greater chaos. But that possibility would assume that the current government does nothing or performs worse than the Chiluba regime in addressing the current social ills including widespread corruption, poverty, and hunger. In fact, it would be a tall order for any Zambian government today to perform worse than that previous regime. At the moment, we have already witnessed some signs of a strong policy to deal with official corruption. We have also seen efforts, albeit weak and disjointed, to address poverty, respond to the hunger crisis, and fight HIV/AIDS. Therefore the pointers are that the Mwanawasa administration, while lacking the capacity to do better, could barely hold the line to maintain the status quo and thereby avert further social deterioration into an irreversible chaos.

On the other hand, the third scenario envisages that Zambia, guided by a sound leadership and given its boundless resources, could recover and achieve social progress. But that would entail, first and foremost, a more robust "melting pot" of public policy activism that is still missing. By this I mean that Zambia would need the formation of political and policy partnerships between government and opposition parties and civil society organizations including labor, business, and the religious community to fashion a more coherent national program, a more focused consensus around a truly common agenda. Would that call for the constitution of a government of national unity or the convening of a broad-based national conference to draw up a recovery program? Fine, as long as society would be able to reach a credible common agenda, followed by the launch of an emergency recovery program, a radical reordering of national priorities, a frontal assault on the structures of poverty, and the establishment of clear targets and timetables for program delivery. Given the magnitude of the current Zambian crises, that is what the country needs—a true multiparty melting pot, a synthesis of ideas, policies, and skills. It would thus be imperative to extract workable ideas from the manifestos of those parties that contested the elections and put them into action on the ground. And, more importantly, the national talent—professionals with expertise to develop the country—also needs to be pooled from all political parties and from Zambians both at home and abroad to assist in the rebuilding exercise. Zambia cannot and will not develop without its best-trained, most-talented nationals to steer the ship to social progress.

In the final analysis, we need to draw lessons from such a critical national event as the 2001 Zambian elections. If there is one lesson to be learned from those elections, judged from the intensity and passions they engendered, it is that whenever stakes are high, people often rise to the occasion to exercise the country's best minds. The best intellectual and professional minds can ill-afford to be idle onlookers in elections like that, or to serve as armchair critics standing on the sidelines, those who American President Harry S. Truman once described as "timid souls who know neither victory nor defeat." It is time for everyone to get involved in the rebuilding of Zambia. Personally, I was mightily disappointed by the lack of involvement by the Zambian intellectuals and professionals in those crucial elections to determine the country's destiny in the twenty-first century. I hold a firm conviction, like Plato's, that the true meaning of citizenship in a democratic society is active participation in its public affairs. The words of the late U.S. Senator Robert F. Kennedy are instructive here: "Pleasantries, self-satisfied mediocrity, will serve us badly. We need the best of many—not just a few. We must strive for excellence." With the twenty-first century now upon us, and Zambians still wallowing in extreme poverty and social injustice, it is imperative to seek leadership of government as the platform through which to inspire our people and make bold decisions that affect destinies of generations of Zambians, ours and those yet to come. That is why I ran for president of Zambia.

INTRODUCTION

Eradication of poverty is essential to consolidate the gains of our new democracy. It is a precondition for social justice, peace and security in our land ... Poverty is about lack of access, lack of power, lack of income and resources to make choices and take advantage of opportunities.

Declaration of War on Poverty—
by the South African Civil Society, August 1997

There are 400 multimillionaires with more wealth than half the world's population. It is an invitation to conflict.... We need leaders who possess a clear vision, who can take on the real challenges that put the peace and security of our planet at risk: poverty, injustice, illiteracy, disease, environmental degradation, drugs.

Oscar Arias, former president of
Costa Rica and 1997 Nobel Peace Laureate

At the end of the century, which has seen unparalleled advances in political freedom, poverty still burdens the lives of millions who live in our region, our continent and indeed the world. That is an indictment of the past from which we are emerging.

Nelson Mandela, former president of
South Africa and 1992 Nobel Peace Laureate

Poverty, peace, and development are intertwined and self-reinforcing concepts. Extreme poverty undermines peace, and the absence of peace constrains development. Every individual in society yearns to live in peace, free to exercise fundamental rights and freedoms and to enjoy the benefits of development. Extreme poverty severely limits the individual's capacity to exercise or enjoy those freedoms and rights. Southern Africa is a region of contrasts; ostentatious wealth coexists with grinding poverty that deprives millions of citizens of their rights to peace, human security, development, and social progress.

This book seeks to accomplish three overriding objectives: first, to examine the complex issues of poverty, peace, and development, their causes, manifestations, dimensions, and consequences in the context of Southern Africa, and the related public policy implications to mitigate them. The second objective is to highlight and assess the public policy interventions and performance—the successes or failures of programs to reduce poverty and promote development—in the post-colonial, post-conflict, and post-apartheid periods. The final objective is to outline some policy proposals and recommendations regarding strategies and institutional reforms necessary to reverse impoverishment in the region and improve the human condition.

The study draws substantially on the presentations and empirical evidence gathered during two 1997 UN regional forums on poverty organized by the UN Information Centres that were held in Windhoek, Namibia, and Midrand, South Africa. Those activities demonstrated that poverty was pervasive throughout the region and that national policies had failed to exert meaningful impact on its alleviation and reduction of human suffering. That knowledge was subsequently updated and expanded in spring 2000, following my teaching of a course on the political economy of poverty and development in Southern Africa at the School of International and Public Affairs of Columbia University. The course provided useful feedback that compelled the revision of some of the data and concepts presented here. Furthermore, the manuscript was revised and expanded in the summer of 2004 to include some reflections on the issues raised during my campaign for president of Zambia in the 2001 elections, as well as to capture new developments regarding the land crisis in Zimbabwe and peace movements in Angola.

The analysis demonstrates, however, that in spite of the region's abundant resources, Southern Africa continues to falter on the development front. It still faces monumental challenges: military conflicts continue to simmer in Angola and the DRC with devastating spill-over consequences, levels of unemployment remain high, inequalities in the distribution of wealth persist, and chronic hunger, malnutrition, crime, violence, and political avarice have inflicted human casualties and dashed the hopes and dreams of the region's inhabitants.

THE SCOPE

Southern Africa means an area covering the Southern African Development Community (SADC), a regional grouping comprising fourteen countries with a vast territory of approximately 480 million hectares of land area. It has an estimated population of well over 190 million.[1] More than 70 percent of the region's people are rural, earning their livelihood directly from subsistence agriculture, and the vast majority of them poor.

The region is home to six of the world's poorest, so-called least developed countries, including Angola, Lesotho, Malawi, Mozambique, Tanzania, and Zambia. However, significant disparities exist in the levels of economic development among and within the countries of the region. Estimated incomes per capita (in U.S. dollars) range from as high as $3,380 for the island nation of Mauritius to as low as $80 for Mozambique, $120 for Tanzania, $170 for Malawi, and $400 each for Zambia and Angola. South Africa's per capita income of $3,160 is forty times higher than that of neighboring Mozambique. It is no wonder that throughout recent history there have been intense drifts of migrant labor from poorer to richer countries of the region, destined more especially for South Africa.

Critical also are the glaring socioeconomic contradictions or disparities within the countries of the region. While islands of wealth exist within a few urban centers—Johannesburg, Cape Town, Harare, Gaborone, Maputo, Lusaka, and others—the vast sea of the outlying rural areas, home to millions of the inhabitants, lies desolate, unproductive, and often neglected. The poverty burden of the Gauteng Province of South Africa, the country's industrial heartland, for example, is nowhere comparable to the crippling squalor afflicting the 5,000 inhabitants of Mier community in the country's Northern Cape Province, or the residents of the former *Bantustans* or homelands of Transkei and Ciskei in the Eastern Cape Province, or even the people of Burgersdorp in the impoverished Gazankulu of the Northern Province. In those outlying areas, the manifestations of extreme poverty, including hunger, unemployment, malnutrition, illiteracy, disease, and even death, are a daily occurrence.

While less than one third of the residents of Gaborone in Botswana lives in poverty, the people of the entire San culture in the remote settlement of New Xade in the central Kalahari live under the most squalid conditions and face extinction. There, the San people still cling to a life of depression, desperation, and hunger, marginalized from modernity; they are now beginning to lose the staple food of roasting desert squash.

Typically, poverty entraps and destroys millions of rural households throughout the remote areas of Southern Africa, from the Katule village of Masvingo in southern Zimbabwe, to Nchilenge district of northern Zambia, to Ovitoto in northern Namibia. Here, the poor bear the brunt of mass unemployment, illiteracy, and physical isolation from the spheres of policy, power, and development. Thus, to rural inhabitants in Southern Africa, poverty implies a high risk of dying prematurely in childbirth, of malnutrition and hunger, or of preventable and treatable diseases including malaria.

THE CREDO

In the post-colonial and post-apartheid Southern Africa, I believe poverty is now the number-one enemy and threat to peace, human security, and social stability. It portends ominously and could thwart the democratic transformation currently under way in the region. In October 1997, junior Zambian military officers cited poverty as the primary motivation for the attempted coup d'état. It is poverty that led to thousands of Zimbabwean protesters taking to the streets of Harare in an outcry against price increases for food and other essential commodities. In recent months, driven by unbearable poverty, Zimbabwe's poor have engaged in land invasions to settle on white-owned commercial farms, thereby completely depressing agricultural production in the country. Poverty and mass unemployment have pushed former veterans of the liberation struggles in South Africa, Namibia, and Zimbabwe to protests in order to highlight their plight. They feel marginalized from the social prosperity that they fought for. And, by and large, the rising crime wave in the region has been largely attributable to poverty, as former young warriors who were taught to wield weapons of war now find the opportunities of peace they fought for closed to them. They lack any other skills for gaining livelihood and have to struggle desperately to find means of survival on a daily basis. Poverty is likewise at the root of official corruption including bribery, graft, and fraud that have ravaged societies. Housing schemes were swindled in Namibia, and high-profile cabinet officials were accused of drug trafficking and other crimes in Zambia. Zimbabwe was recently rocked by fraudulent land redistribution deals by senior officials. In

South Africa, police officers have given shelter to crime rackets that injure the very public they are charged to protect.

Meanwhile, the inhabitants of the region must remain vigilant against the politics of poverty, albeit the poverty of politics being exercised throughout the region. It is poverty, for instance, that causes those who have ruled their countries for decades to continue to desperately cling onto power or to seek third, fourth, or fifth terms in office, as demonstrated in the recent Namibian and Zimbabwean cases. At the same time, those voted out of power, as was former president Kenneth Kaunda of Zambia in 1991, still want to fight to recapture their lost glory or to sponsor their children to do so. Because of poverty, it appears that corruption is being sanctioned at higher levels directly by elected officials. Poverty considerations recently motivated elected members of parliament in Namibia to justify voting in advance for their own huge retirement packages while still in office. Similarly, because of poverty, Zambian members of parliament also voted for huge increases in their seating gratuities and allowances to purchase new vehicles for themselves. The most troubling aspect about such officially sanctioned acts of greed was that they were done without any social conscience. Elected officials cannot afford to arrogantly turn a blind eye to the hundreds of thousands of their wretchedly poverty-stricken electorate, those who must struggle day in and day out just to survive to the next day. Clearly, we need to confront and curb such greed-driven public policy in the region.

WHY BOTHER ABOUT THE POOR?

That intriguing question was first posed by Sir Shridal Ramphal, former secretary general of the Commonwealth, in his poignant assessment of abject poverty amid much opulence gripping the newly democratic South Africa. He observed that apartheid had answered the question rather surgically. "It did so directly and brutally," he concluded, "don't bother about the many who are poor ... except as instruments for the few who are rich."[2]

That underlying socioeconomic dichotomy is still a reality in Southern Africa. In post-apartheid South Africa, Namibia and, to a large extent, Zimbabwe, promoting social justice is compelling social imperative. It poses a real human problem and imposes an obligation on the social polity to intervene. South Africa and Namibia have among the most progressive constitutions in the world. While those instruments have helped to shape the agenda for development from the *political* realm that has already been realized, they must now hasten the pursuit of *social justice* that is yet to be fulfilled. In reality "the political" and "the economic" imperatives must now converge in their social application to improve human life. The issues of wealth, its distribution, and social justice juxtapose and need to be pursued concurrently and reconciled in a democratic environment. Democracy comes with social responsibilities and obligations to apply political power to exercise fairness in society, combat poverty, empower the people, and guarantee their well-being.

- Governments in Southern African should, therefore, bother or care deeply about the poor because combating poverty is a democratic imperative necessary to improve the human condition of the vast majority of the people. If democracy is a concept of numbers, which it is, then public policy should not allow the vast majority of the people of any country to be trapped in extreme poverty and denied full participation in political and economic life. The greater the country's population involved in its economic life and production of national wealth, the larger the number of people who would benefit from its distribution and, in turn, the greater the enhancement of peace and social stability.

- We must bother about the poor because absolute poverty offends the human sense of justice and equity. Compassion and social justice demand that society cannot leave millions of fellow citizens to wallow in extreme hunger, malnutrition, and deprivation amid abundance. For a healthier society, development demands a broader distribution of economic and productive assets including land, more equitable access to opportunities, and an end to discrimination on account of race, gender, or other extraneous factors.

- Leadership must bother about the poor because poverty, extreme wealth and income inequalities, mass unemployment, and the lack of access to opportunities constitute an inefficient allocation of resources and potential source of conflict in society. To reduce poverty and glaring inequalities in the distribution of opportunities requires greater popular participation and optimum utilization of national resources including land and labor.

- Society needs to be concerned about the poor because development is a human rights imperative. Article 25 of the Universal Declaration of Human Rights entrenched the rights of every person to food, shelter, and basic social services. As a result, women, children, indigenous societies, the elderly, and the disabled have lately become protected species under various international conventions, covenants, and protocols, making it an obligation of states to uplift their citizens from conditions of abject poverty, want, and squalor.

- Governments must care about the poor because economically, they constitute the bedrock of the creation of national wealth. In country after country in Southern Africa, including in those few with relative prosperity, the poor have labored hard to build the national industrial structures, construct the infrastructure, and build homes; to dig out gold, diamonds, and copper; to produce food and raise families. The poor, therefore, deserve to share in the prosperity of the nation as partners and active agents in any programs intended to improve their well-being.

- We must seriously address human poverty because the alleviation of human suffering promotes peace, strengthens the social fabric, enhances popular participation, and ensures political and economic stability in society. Poor communities engaged in national development acquire a stake in the society and promote its preservation, while those marginalized or alienated from it do not.

- Finally, the people of Southern Africa must care deeply about the poor and least endowed citizens because the reduction of extreme poverty and elimination of social disparities would enhance a broader sense of community, the common destiny that SADC strives to fashion in this new millennium, a period of infinite promise for greater integration and social progress.

To address these challenges, chapter 1 sketches a broader, historical framework for the poverty debate. It examines some of the root causes and consequences of poverty in the region, including the investment bias against the rural sector, impact of armed conflicts, lack of peace, population dislocations, the refugee burden, as well as the debt crisis and economic mismanagement facing the countries of the region. Chapter 2 delves into an analysis of basic needs and human development. It establishes yardsticks for policy intervention and performance in poverty reduction or eradication. Although all countries of the region staked out policy positions at the 1995 Copenhagen World Summit for Social Development, few have matched their words with deeds to implement that global consensus. Countries like Angola and Mozambique have been overwhelmed by conflicts and thus have lagged far behind in the provisioning of basic social needs.

The critical linkages between poverty, peace, and transformation are examined and analysed in chapter 3. I argue that peace in the present context is more than just the absence of war; it must be the removal of the causes of conflicts as well. It has been demonstrated that extreme poverty is a real threat to peace and social stability. Poor security personnel, armies of unemployed veterans of liberation wars or school leavers, landless peasants, as well as underpaid and homeless domestic and farm workers cannot remain peaceful for long. Public policy must intervene vigorously to bring relief to their plight.

Also critically important in Southern Africa are issues of gender discrimination, gender balance, and gender-sensitive programming of resources, especially in dealing with problems affecting rural women. With more than 70 percent of the region's population still rural and rural women bearing the brunt of absolute poverty and its consequences of illiteracy, malnutrition, unemployment, domestic violence, death in childbirth, and of HIV/AIDS infections, pursuit of gender equality must take center stage. Therefore, chapter 4 focuses on the gender questions and demonstrates that while some states fare better than others in gender issues, none can claim to have adequately addressed, with any policy consistency, matters specifically relating to the upliftment of rural women. Chapter 5 explores more vigorously the underlying issues of policy interventions under various social paradigms by examining the politico-economic determinants at country levels. Policy interventions have varied from country to country and depended on the resource endowments of the countries concerned. One fact, however, remains indisputable: extreme human poverty and social deprivation in any country impose dire consequences on the entire region. Hence, there is a pressing need to adopt a more coherent regional strategy, a common agenda of combating human poverty.

Finally, chapter 6 is prescriptive. It focuses on some of the strategic practicalities of public policy interventions required to bring about social relief and improvement in the living conditions of the people of Southern Africa. I contend that poverty can only be alleviated, reduced, and eventually eradicated in an environment of peace, where economic growth comes with equity and social protections, where people's access to critical assets (including land) is guaranteed, and where the pursuit of social justice becomes the centerpiece of the development agenda. Anything short of this is a betrayal of the people's aspirations for a better life. And acting singularly, public policy will continue to falter in mitigating poverty. What is required is a broad-based, region-wide collaborative agenda that fosters social networks and partnerships between governments, civil society, and the poor themselves to tackle the critical issues of the moment—poverty, access, justice, and social progress. Political elites must now come down from their ivory towers to begin to work with grassroots organizations to promote a common development agenda. Poverty reduction and its eventual eradication can be achieved only if there are political will and commitment for affirmative, proactive policy measures taken at the highest levels of national government to uplift those at the bottom of the development scale.

CHAPTER ONE:

THE HISTORICAL CONTEXT — ROOTS OF POVERTY IN SOUTHERN AFRICA

It is paradoxical that a region so abundantly endowed with natural resources should be among the poorest, afflicted with grinding poverty. The late president of Botswana Seretse Khama put it succinctly: "We have within our borders ... the raw materials for industrialization—energy and base metals. We have energy in the form of oil, coal, uranium, hydroelectric power and of course limitless solar energy when it can be harnessed; and we have base metals such as iron, copper, nickel, cobalt, chrome, lead, and zinc. Add to these our diamonds and gold and the wide variety of our agricultural products including cotton, sisal, tea, coffee, tobacco, sugar, wool, maize, wheat, leather, beef, woodpulp and mohair."[1] He appealed for collective political will to promote intra-regional trade, cooperation, and economic development under the then Southern African Development Coordination Conference (SADCC), the forerunner of the present SADC.

With such bountiful resources, conflicts abated, and apartheid finally gone, the region's development potential could now be realized. Some inhibiting factors, however, still persist. They include the inherited colonial legacies, the vestiges of devastating anti-colonial and anti-apartheid conflicts, internal strife that rocked post-independence Angola and Mozambique, the impact of droughts, floods, and other natural disasters as well as land hunger that also plagued the region. With the vast majority of the inhabitants residing in rural areas and earning their livelihood directly from the land, the neglect of agriculture and the rural economy has precipitated severe and widespread poverty. Poverty manifests itself in hunger, malnutrition, ill-health, and low life expectancy. Today, one third of Lesotho's families, 50 percent of Mozambique's population, over 60 percent of Angola's and Zambia's people, as well as some 40 percent of the populations of Zimbabwe and South Africa, especially in rural areas, are malnourished. Malnutrition is most severe among rural women, children under five, the elderly, crippled miners, and other disabled individuals.

This chapter highlights some of the underlying causes of underdevelopment and poverty in Southern Africa, including (1) the legacies of colonial policies that impoverished rural areas by rendering them as pools of cheap labor and vulnerable mono-cultural economies; (2) protracted armed conflicts in the region; (3) economic dependence on hostile apartheid South Africa and the effects of destabilization; (4) impact of the refugee burden; (5) economic crisis of the 1980s exacerbated by the debt burden, economic mismanagement, and public corruption; and (6) preoccupation with political survival instead of summoning political will and determination to combat poverty at any cost.

COLONIAL LEGACIES

Colonialism and imperialism in Southern Africa were first and foremost economic forces with political overtones. Colonization was driven by economic motives with political institutions created largely to consolidate the external stranglehold over the raw materials of the region. In South Africa, Namibia, and Zimbabwe, the settler economies were particularly predominant, and more entrenched, precipitating the most exploitative and segregative sociopolitical structures, with the most extreme brand being apartheid in South Africa. Apartheid in South Africa and Namibia invented the extreme forms of segregation in space settlement and provision of social services never before witnessed. It was an advanced stage of the state's attempt to exercise political and legal power to marginalize the majority black population while guaranteeing social benefits and wealth to the white minority.

The investment contradictions were glaring. Colonial investment was attracted to the region mainly by the glitter of gold and diamonds. Countries were encouraged to concentrate primarily on the expansion of the extractive export sector, including the production of mineral, agricultural, and other primary products for international trade.[2]

That orthodox investment approach was premised on the principle that the response to market demands for raw materials by the growing industrial complexes of Europe and elsewhere would create an intrinsic relationship between those external markets and the development of local economies. The local economies, made so totally dependent on the export sector and primary production, were expected to generate the capital and foreign exchange earnings required for investment in the economic infrastructure, industry, agriculture, and social activities. It was assumed that such a pattern of foreign investment would promote a form of partnership between the investors and the states concerned in the exploitation of raw materials whereby foreign investors, particularly in the mining and similar extractive sectors, would bring capital and managerial skills, and local economies would provide the required natural resources, policy guidance, cheap labor, and other incentives. In the end, according to that argument, all concerned would mutually benefit; investors would reap huge returns on their capital and host countries would create employment opportunities, generate revenues and foreign exchange earnings, and enhance other possibilities through the multiplier effect to the local economies.[3]

That development scenario, however, largely failed to materialize. As it turned out, the very preponderance of minerals and other extractive sectors in the region militated against balanced development of the local economies. While South Africa and Zimbabwe developed more diversified economic structures than the rest of the region, this analysis demonstrates that their development was driven and ultimately skewed by the predominance of the settler populations.

Foreign capital was first attracted to Southern Africa through the South African Witwatersrand and Kimberley diamond and gold mining ventures of the 1870s. The development of Kimberley diamond mines coincided with economic expansion in Europe. While European capital was aggressively seeking new investment opportunities in the region, Kimberley was also looking for more financing to develop its mines and exert influence to the north beyond the South African frontiers. Consequently, major diamond and later gold investors strengthened the links between Southern Africa and the European capital markets.[4]

The famous goldfield of Zimbabwe, once thought to be one of the biblical King Solomon's sources of riches, attracted the explorer Cecil John Rhodes to form his British South African Company to spearhead investment in mineral development. He later realized, however, that mineral deposits of Zimbabwe had been grossly overestimated, as neither gold nor diamonds existed on the same scale as those in South Africa. Gold production peaked in the early 1900s, and it was that extensive search for gold and diamonds that led to the discovery of other metals in Zimbabwe including chrome, nickel, copper, asbestos, and coal. By that period, over 70 percent of all private capital flow from Europe was directed to Southern Africa and devoted directly to the development of mineral-producing activities of gold and diamond in South Africa; diamonds in Namibia; copper, lead, and zinc in Zambia; gold, asbestos, and coal in Zimbabwe; and diamonds in Angola.[5]

Ironically, that colonial thrust on mineral development failed to capacitate the local economies to achieve self-sufficiency, balanced national development, or the production of adequate basic food requirements. Instead, that pattern of externally driven, skewed development largely benefited the urban enclaves inhabited by the white minority population to the exclusion of the vast majority rural people. It further entrenched the structures of poverty and deprivation, especially in rural areas that prevail today, characterized by extreme inequalities in the distribution of land and national wealth.

This is not to argue, however, that mining did not contribute tangibly to the development of the region. It did immensely. Indeed, mining in many parts of the region became the engine of development of local economies through expansion of the gross domestic product (GDP), generation of government revenue, earning of foreign exchange, and creation of employment opportunities. In the area of employment, mining activities became important magnets of migrant labor throughout the region. In Zambia, for instance, pools of unskilled labor drifted from rural regions to its copperbelt area, and in South Africa, mining centers were the principal attractions of large numbers of migrant workers.[6] Faced with such extreme poverty in the rural areas, the African male of Southern Africa was, as Karl Max so aptly put it, "incessantly" forced to sell his labor power in order to live.[7]

The communications and other infrastructural links took similar patterns of development intended to service the urban mining centers almost exclusively. Better transport and telecommunications were also developed along the same lines. The mining technological requirements were largely imported, in the cases of Angola, Botswana, Zambia and Zimbabwe, directly from Europe or from South Africa; South Africa had the capacity to manufacture its own equipment and to export equipment. Those imports in turn depleted foreign exchange reserves and investment resources. Thus, throughout Southern Africa, mining took the center stage and together with a few urban industrial complexes, consumed large amounts of investment capital, transport and communications infrastructure, energy, as well as labor to the exclusion of the rural areas. As a consequence, today extreme rural poverty coexists with islands of wealth in a few urban centers such as Johannesburg, Harare, Gaborone, and Windhoek.

The South African development experience, however, was unique and characterized by many extreme features. With the influx of capital, South Africa developed a complex mining industry based on gold production and built a dynamic and dominant manufacturing heavy industrial sector. These structures developed side by side with a stagnant, subsistence, and poverty-stricken rural economy that served primarily as sources of cheap labor. Thus, apart from foreign investment and skills, the sophisticated South African industrial complex was built on the basis of a massive exploitation of cheap, non-unionized, unskilled, disenfranchised black labor drawn from both within its impoverished rural areas and without its frontiers. The low cost of such labor and the extremely poor working and living conditions of the miners enabled the companies to reap huge profits and to plow the surplus back into further mining and other forms of industrial expansion. The diamond industry had a special characteristic: it did not require large amounts of capital, but it did generate huge profits. The surplus derived from diamonds was plowed into the gold mining of the Transvaal. Meanwhile, as these operations expanded, the rural economy deteriorated further because it had lost most of the young, productive, and energetic male labor that had been forced to drift to the urban mining centers.

Finally, the other critical factor of the South African development scenario was the indigenization of racism by the settler community, which dictated that development would benefit only a narrow segment of the society. From the inception of the investment rush of the nineteenth and twentieth centuries, there was an interplay of racial discrimination and vigorous Afrikaner nationalism that determined the nature and pattern of social exclusion. The capitalist foreign investors and mining companies forged forces and settled in South Africa as local entrepreneurs. That strategy led to the establishment of a political alliance between white miners, other white workers, and the Afrikaner nationalism to culturally unify the investing class that also controlled the state political machinery. That investing group subsequently became part of the ruling class of South Africa and entrenched the settler economy into every economic life from commercialized agriculture to mining and entrepreneurial manufacturing. At the policy level, white South Africans applied the power of the state to extract surplus from the burgeoning mining sector to expand the manufacturing and heavy industrial development as well as to invest massively into the private sector, especially into white social services such as education and skills development. It further provided agricultural loans, grants, and subsidies to infant industries intended to boost productivity. Thus, as the white population of the country prospered, the settler community invested vastly into its own self-interest intended to support social infrastructure for the white minority while, at the same time, depriving the black majority of those basic services. Those same socio-political formations of settler nationalism were subsequently to be extended to Namibia and, to some extent, to Zimbabwe as well.[8]

Armed Conflicts and Apartheid Backlash

For more than three decades, Southern Africa was embroiled in costly and destructive wars against colonialism and apartheid in South Africa, as well as long-running civil conflicts in Angola and Mozambique.[9] Those conflicts caused massive population, community, and economic dislocations throughout the region. Millions of people became displaced, internally and externally, and often crowded the marginal areas of squatter settlements on the urban fringes. Those disturbances further aggravated population demands for food, water, fuel, and social services.[10]

The oppressed people of Southern Africa waged anti-colonial and anti-apartheid wars to gain sovereignty over their resources and to exact social justice.[11] While Tanzania, Zambia, Malawi, Botswana, Lesotho, Swaziland, and Mauritius gained political independence through negotiations, the struggle for the liberation of Angola, Mozambique, Zimbabwe, Namibia, and South Africa saw violent armed confrontations and much bloodshed.

Angola and Mozambique were among the first to launch military operations against Portuguese colonialism. The Popular Movement for the Liberation of Angola (MPLA) began its campaign in 1961. It was subsequently joined by the National Front for the Liberation of Angola (FNLA) and the National Union for the Total Independence of Angola (UNITA). On the Mozambican front, the Front for the Liberation of Mozambique (FRELIMO) led the liberation struggle. The organizations launched their operations against the Portuguese military installations from Tanzania, Zambia, and, to some extent, from the DRC.[12]

With regard to Zimbabwe, the Zimbabwe African National Union-Patriotic Front (ZANU-PF) and the Zimbabwe African People's Union-Patriotic Front (ZAPU-PF) spearheaded that struggle for independence. Both organizations mounted formidable military operations against the Rhodesian forces from bases in Zambia and Mozambique.[13]

The African National Congress (ANC) and the South West Africa People's Organization (SWAPO) prosecuted the freedom struggle for South Africa and Namibia internally and externally, respectively. They spearheaded military operations from bases located mainly in Zambia, Angola, and Mozambique and were supported internally by allied civil society organizations, primarily the labor movements and religious community.[14] ANC, which began the anti-colonial campaign in 1912, was banned in South Africa following the upheavals of the treason trials of the 1950s and 1960s. It went underground and eventually into exile. With its leaders underground, exiled, or imprisoned, ANC abandoned its nonviolent protests and took up arms against the apartheid regime.[15]

The South African presence in Namibia dates back to the colonial period of the imperial Germany. Since then, South Africa's intrusion into Namibia was extensive, eclipsing the crucial spheres of investment in mining, transport, and other services. It so dominated Namibia's economy to the point that German businesses of the time had to mount protests against South Africa.[16] Ironically, the conferring of the League of Nations Mandate over Namibia to South Africa to administer it as a "sacred trust," instead served to make South Africa's colonial grip on the territory harsher in an effort to annex it. South Africa dominated Namibia's political and economic life and ruthlessly repressed, impoverished, and exploited its population and vast natural resources.[17] Thus SWAPO and ANC coordinated their prosecution of the war, political mobilization, and international campaigns against apartheid South Africa. The SWAPO's first military operation against the South African forces took place at Ongulumbatshe in northern Namibia in August 1966, and its campaign intensified during the 1970s and 1980s. This led to the apartheid regime's declaration in the 1980s of a "total onslaught" on the people of South Africa, Namibia, and the region, marking the beginning of nearly two decades of extraordinary internal repression, massive destruction, and destabilization of the region.[18]

The extraordinarily fierce resistance mounted by the settlers in what was then Rhodesia, apartheid South Africa, and occupied Namibia was the result of their well-entrenched political, economic, and military power. In the desperate attempt to thwart the liberation tide to the north, apartheid South Africa flexed its economic and military muscle and devised a grand design of serving as a surrogate state for the protection of Western economic and cold war interests in the region against nationalist (labeled communist) threats. As a result, it lashed out on its northern neighbors and became engaged in a range of conflicts and counteroffensives both prior to and after the demise of colonialism in Angola, Mozambique, and Zimbabwe. Apartheid South Africa's destabilization campaigns took many fronts including (1) rendering material and military support to the Portuguese and Rhodesian regimes in their fight against nationalist movements, (2) intensification of internal political repression, (3) economic and military blackmail of independent neighboring states, (4) covert operations to assassinate the opponents of apartheid, (5) sponsoring of internal political rebellions or counterinsurgents in the neighboring states, and (6) direct military interventions into Angola and occupation of Namibia.

Southern Africa has always harbored extensive South African and Western economic interests that South Africa claimed to protect. Despite some localization, South African and Western transnational corporations and financial institutions that controlled the capital, skills, and technology in particular dominated the extractive sectors. The South African Anglo-American Corporation, for example, had vast investments and interests in the diamond mines of Angola and Botswana, power and energy projects in Mozambique, copper mining in Zambia, gold mining, agricultural estates, and industrial development of Zimbabwe, coal mining of Swaziland and others. Obviously, South Africa intended to defend the colonial structures that protected those interests. Clearly, continued Portuguese colonial presence in Angola and Mozambique and a minority rule in Rhodesia (Zimbabwe) were very much in South Africa's interest to provide political and security buffers between itself and the independent countries in the north. South Africa also recognized that military victories by the anti-colonial movements in the north would trigger a domino effect on South Africa's own internal apartheid-colonial situation.

For those reasons, South Africa provided substantial material and logistical support to the Portuguese military activities in Angola and Mozambique, as well as to the then Rhodesian forces. The South African and Portuguese military cooperated to provide protection of the Angolan diamond mines and its Cabinda oil fields that were under constant guerrilla threats. Similarly, in Mozambique, the Cabora Bassa hydroelectric project, which was developed by the Anglo-American consortium to provide power from Mozambique to South Africa, represented another centerpiece of the Portuguese-South African defense pact.

Internally, South Africa intensified its repression of the civilian population. Not since the treason trials and Sharpeville uprisings and massacre of the 1950s and 1960s had the country gone through so much political turmoil as it did during the 1970s and 1980s. In its attempt to suppress the Soweto school protests of 1976 against the inferior Bantu education and the imposition of Afrikaans as the language of instruction, South African forces massacred some 4,000 schoolchildren. Meanwhile, Steven Biko's new Black Consciousness Movement of the 1970s served to galvanize the youth to resist apartheid in schools, churches, and workplaces. Later, the South African Council of Churches, the United Democratic Front (UDF), the Congress of South African Trade Unions (COSATU), and a wide spectrum of civil society organizations joined in the mass agitation to end the apartheid system in South Africa and to free political prisoners, including Nelson Mandela.

Thus, throughout the 1980s, the apartheid regime was on the defensive and mounted an aggressive assault on anti-apartheid campaigners. The Council of Churches headquarters in Johannesburg was bombed and destroyed by the so-called "White Wolves," a state-sponsored right-wing organization. Some media publications were also banned, with editors and labor union leaders detained and imprisoned.[19] In Namibia, the struggle was equally intense as the religious community and labor leaders took a more active role. As political pressure for change mounted on apartheid South Africa, the regime's repression became more vicious and its security forces more destructive. In Namibia, South African security forces began to destroy rural communities and refugee settlements, culminating in the May 1978 Kassinga massacre of some 600 Namibian refugees at a camp in southern Angola.[20]

Dependence and Apartheid Destabilization

As far back as the 1960s, apartheid South Africa was already a dominant political and economic power in Southern Africa and a staunch opponent of political liberation. With such a dominant hostile neighbor, there was little chance that newly independent and tiny countries such as Botswana, Lesotho, and Swaziland (BLS) would realistically chart an independent course to mitigate poverty or achieve sustainable development. The long-range strategy for South Africa, however, was to enhance its strangulation of those states through such vital spheres as trade, transport, and communications; food security; employment; energy and power; and, more importantly, to control the political and security agenda of the region.

Virtually all countries of the region were severely dependent on South Africa for their vital survival but none more so than the BLS states, which were practically hostages in every respect. Six of the countries of the region—the BLS states plus Malawi, Zambia, and Zimbabwe—were landlocked and conducted their international trade largely through South Africa. Thus Zambia and Zimbabwe and, to a large extent, even coastal Mozambique were also dependent on South Africa in transport, trade, and other vital areas.[21] Although the exact nature and scope of dependence varied from country to country, approximately 90 percent of all BLS imports came from or through South Africa, including 50 percent of foodstuff. Apart from the BLS countries, Malawi, Mozambique, and Zimbabwe also had significant amounts of import requirements coming from or through South Africa.[22]

Food security was severely compromised due to the region's extreme dependence on hostile South Africa. Half of the food requirements consumed in the BLS states and significant amounts of food supplies for Mozambique and Zambia were imported from South Africa. Thus, throughout the 1980s, those five states continued to import large amounts of food from or through apartheid South Africa. Apart from South Africa, only Zimbabwe was the other net exporter of cereal and meat products to the neighboring countries. Overall, poor food supplies and hefty import costs had the consequence of serious nutritional deficiencies among the region's population. In that regard, even in South Africa, poverty, suffering, and malnutrition were quite severe especially in the so-called black homelands.[23]

With regard to employment dependence on South Africa, some 86 percent of Lesotho's, 50 percent of Botswana's, 20 percent of Swaziland's, and approximately 15 percent each of Malawi's and Mozambique's wage earners were employed in South African mining industrial complexes. The financial remittances from those migrant workers constituted significant portions of the GDP of their home countries and also provided much-needed foreign exchange. However, at the height of political conflicts in the latter part of 1980s into the early 1990s, South Africa suddenly began the repatriation of some foreign migrant workers in order to absorb its own growing surplus workforce from the Transkei and Ciskei homelands. Moreover, South Africa also became increasingly fearful that foreign labor from independent northern neighbors would politically radicalize its own domestic workforce to agitate against the unjust laws of the apartheid state.[24]

Energy and power dependence on South Africa, particularly among the BLS countries, was almost total. Those countries also heavily depended on South Africa for oil and electricity supplies. Mozambique, on the other hand, possessed vast gas reserves that were still exploited. Meanwhile, however, its Cabora Bassa hydroelectric project was designed to export all of its energy output to South Africa because its grid did not provide access to other countries of the region. Angola, on the other hand, was the only other country that could export some petroleum products from its vast Cabinda oil fields. However, its oil output was on the decline in the 1980s as a result of the South African and UNITA military activities.[25] Zambia and Zimbabwe were by the 1970s self-sufficient in electric power supplies from the Kariba dam and Kafue gorge projects. Zambia was in fact a net exporter of electric power to Zimbabwe in the south and the Congolese mines to the north.

With respect to the financial and monetary sectors, links with South Africa were especially strong among the BLS countries that belonged to the South African Customs Union (SACU) and, except for Botswana, to the Rand Monetary Area as well. Overall in the region, the power of South African capital was pervasive. Many banks, financial institutions, and firms operating in the BLS and other neighboring countries were subsidiaries of South African companies and had their headquarters based directly in South Africa. The South African–based Anglo-American Corporation, for instance, held mining concerns and other ventures throughout the region. It was also estimated that the total value of the Anglo-American associated companies was equivalent to US$7 billion in 1980, amounting to resources many times larger than the GDP of most countries of the region.[26] With such a vast imbalance in economic power, any negotiations for industrial localization between Anglo-American and independent African countries was to the disadvantage of the weak countries. Under the circumstances, the countries of the region were unable to adopt or pursue truly independent public policies designed to enhance social development. Thus South Africa was able to apply its political, economic, and military power to intimidate or destabilize at will its weak neighbors.

REFUGEE BURDEN

One measure of the destruction caused by the armed conflicts was the massive refugee influx in the region. At the peak of the fighting in the late 1970s to mid-1980s, some 3.5 million people were on the move, fleeing from the war zones of Angola, Mozambique, Namibia, Zimbabwe, and South Africa to seek sanctuary in the neighboring countries and elsewhere. Millions more people had been displaced internally. By 1988, for instance, refugees from Mozambique alone had exceeded one million, and another half million had been uprooted from Angola. Malawi, Zimbabwe, Tanzania, and Swaziland, among them, hosted around 1.3 million Mozambican refugees. Meanwhile, hundreds of thousands more refugees fled from Namibia and South Africa to settle in camps in Angola, Botswana and Zambia.[27]

Refugees by their very nature were unsettled populations and therefore largely unproductive and poor. They survived on public charge, consuming whatever was available and often had little or nothing to eat. As expected, the energetic youths constituted almost half of the refugee populations, of which three quarters were women and children. Those were also some of the most vulnerable groups to the catastrophes of mass unemployment, hunger, malnutrition, and diseases. Moreover, such influxes of refugees were also disruptive to the local economies of both the countries of origin and destination countries. Massive depopulation, especially of the rural areas, resulted in the loss of energetic and most productive young labor, thereby severely reducing the productive capacity of the country. At the same time, the receiving countries became severely constrained in social resources such as shortages of food, water, and land, as well as in overburdened educational and health-care services. Thus the refugee crisis in the region, which was at the time estimated to amount to 10 percent of the global refugee population, had an adverse impact on development.[28] As a result, the absolute poverty, especially the wretched squalor prevailing in rural Angola and Mozambique, was directly linked to protracted conflicts, disruptions of large segments of the population, and the resulting refugee situation.

Debt, Mismanagement, and Corruption

During the 1980s, Southern African economies experienced monumental crises resulting from (1) the accumulation of heavy external debt whose repayment devoured large amounts of valuable resources, (2) application of inappropriate policies including the merciless adoption of structural adjustment programs (SAPs), and (3) rampant levels of official corruption, graft, and economic mismanagement.

By the late 1980s, the African external debt situation was economically debilitating.[29] The crisis was compounded largely by declining commodity prices and export earnings that coincided with sharp increases in international interest rates on debt owed. Zambia alone had by 1989 borrowed heavily to the tune of $7.2 billion, more than twice the size of its GDP.[30] It became one of the highly indebted poor countries with burgeoning bureaucracies of an incompetently managed public sector. The country could not even afford the repayment of arrears accumulated on that debt due to its declining export earnings from copper. As a result, Zambia's economy plummeted, people's standards of living declined rapidly, and the population slipped into extreme human poverty.

Similarly, Zimbabwe's debt in 1989 had amounted to $3 billion in just nine years of its independence. Botswana ($515 million), Lesotho ($323 million), Malawi ($1.4 billion), and Mozambique ($5 billion) became equally overcommitted given the sizes of their economies.[31] Zimbabwe's problems were compounded by the country's highly unequal distribution of land, wealth, and income. Landlessness among peasant farmers and unemployment, especially among the demobilized freedom fighters, also escalated. The country was further bedeviled by unchecked official corruption that undermined efforts to develop or manage an otherwise well-endowed economy. Thus conditions of poverty were deep and widespread in the country, especially in rural areas.

Angola and Mozambique also borrowed heavily, primarily for the purpose of sustaining their war efforts. Malawi's debt also escalated mainly to prop up the Kamuzu Banda dictatorial regime that had muzzled that country's civil liberties and democratic freedoms. Apartheid South Africa also accumulated debt amounting to between

$10 billion and $15 billion, resources largely committed to prosecuting its war in defense of the apartheid system internally and externally.

The development impact of debt was devastating on the social and economic well-being of the region. In the struggle to repay debt, especially the mounting interest, poor countries concentrated almost exclusively on the income-generating export sector to the neglect of social investment. The transfer of resources to debt payment seriously eroded the state's capacity for social provisioning. Thus, efforts of governments and local communities to provide essential education, health care, clean water, and sanitation were severely undermined. Secondly, there were hidden costs of debt overhang as the diversion of foreign exchange to external creditors reduced local import capacity. Without those imports, local industries idled, productivity declined, and the national capacity to create employment shrank. Hence rising unemployment and criminality in virtually every country were threats to social stability. Finally, that impact of debt on foreign exchange and the weakening of industrial performance reduced revenues for the poor countries. Obviously, those conditions seriously reduced the state's capacity to provide some of the most essential social and economic requirements such as schoolbooks and hospital drugs.

In addition, the unfettered application of SAPs prescribed by the World Bank and the International Monetary Fund (IMF) imposed severe social costs on the poor. For Zambia, structural adjustment coincided with the collapse in copper prices, foreign exchange scarcity, import decline, and idling of domestic industries. In desperation, the country turned to further borrowing within the SAP framework in an effort to survive.

Theoretically, SAPs were intended to advocate sound public policy measures if such interventions could minimize the social costs on the poor.[32] In essence, SAPs sought to achieve institutional reforms in the microeconomic (taxes and tariffs) and macroeconomic (fiscal) areas of the economy to increase efficiency and expand growth. However, in large measure, the programs had very negative consequences on societies including increased unemployment, reduced social investment, and even more critically, increased food costs for the poor. The unemployment situation was extremely grave in countries where formal-sector employment was already limited and social safety nets were nonexistent. The reduction in government spending further resulted in the collapse of social services, especially education and health care. Finally, SAPs severely weakened the implementation of food security measures. Moves to liberalize the food market and remove controls in an attempt to stimulate production inevitably led to soaring food prices for the poor, the very population already disadvantaged by massive unemployment and cuts in social spending. That state of affairs led to food riots in Zambia in the late 1980s and in Zimbabwe more recently.

The SAPs thus failed to restore sound economic management and stimulate growth. By 1993, the World Bank had identified six SADC countries (Lesotho, Malawi, Namibia, Tanzania, Zambia, and Zimbabwe) as being among the African core group of adjusters—that is, countries that had put in place fairly sound policies and institutional reforms to implement SAPs.[33] However, the performance of those countries, especially in the human development sphere, was disappointing. In Zambia, Zimbabwe, Lesotho, and Malawi, SAPs were associated with major declines in investment, economic growth, and employment opportunities. The better economic performance experienced by Botswana, which was not even included among the World Bank group of core adjusters, was more the result of stability in the governance and disciplined economic policy of the country than the impact of the SAPs.

Rampant public corruption and economic mismanagement have gone hand in glove in destroying the region's capacity to provide basic services to the poor. Corruption has taken the forms of bribery, fraud, graft, and abuse of office, all practices that have undermined good governance and hindered reforms that would directly benefit the poor.

In Zambia, the legacies of graft and drug trafficking by high officials in 1994 quickly weakened the foundations of good governance and reforms that the country sought to institute since the re-establishment of multiparty politics in 1991.[34] The negative impact of corruption, whether by politicians, civil servants, or law-enforcement officials, has been the deepening of poverty resulting from resource diversions and reduced tax revenues to meet public obligations to the poor. Moreover, as the poor were the least able to pay bribes, they could not receive the quality services they deserved. A recent UNDP study warned about the danger of a "disabling state" in which government officials may demand bribes before promoting full access of citizens to public services, and where the well-connected few use political influence to gain preferential access to those services.[35]

A word of caution about the dangers of pervasive statism or the application of government supremacy over everything in the social life of the people and the allocation of resources may be in order here. In Zambia, for instance, the statist policies of wholesale nationalization and public and political party control of enterprises resulted in overexpansion of bureaucracies without adequate management skills to coordinate development. That skill void had to be compensated for by recruiting large numbers of foreign personnel who were assumed to have the abilities to perform the required tasks. Very often, however, expatriate labor did not have the abilities, experience, or cultural commitment to nation-building that development required. In the absence of an effective, centrally directed and managed anti-poverty program, human poverty in Zambia escalated to unprecedented levels. Thus, as it pursued its statist policies, Zambia squandered valuable resources while corruption and nepotism reigned supreme in every public operation, including the ruling party and government. The balance of the resources went into unproductive, grandiose schemes such as the building of new conference centers, new party office complexes, and globe-trotting by the ruling elites. Once again, the poor were the obvious victims.

CONCLUSION

Poverty in the region is not a given but a man-made condition. Human interventions and a new form of political commitment and will can therefore reverse it. The region is well resourced, and yet it is also home to six of the poorest countries in the world. The contributing factors include the extreme bias of colonial investment toward the more profitable extractive mining sector to the neglect of the rural economies. More importantly, the region has not known peace since the 1960s. Protracted armed conflicts have inflicted devastating human casualties, caused much destruction, and constrained development. Poverty also was precipitated by the dependence of states in the region on the hostile apartheid South Africa. Heavily dependent countries became hostages to the apartheid regime's acts of destabilization and blackmail in the critical areas of transport, trade, skills, and employment; they were more preoccupied with disengaging from South Africa than undertaking social investment to combat poverty. The heavy refugee burden, SAPs, economic mismanagement, and official corruption further exacerbated conditions of abject poverty in the region.

Southern Africa cannot endure with a few free while the vast majority of its people are entrapped in the slavery of poverty, facing endless struggle just to survive on a daily basis. There has to be a balance. There has been a realization in the region that poverty, if not mitigated, would destroy the very fabric of the society. However, there are now welcome signs of social activism by civil society organizations and some governments to seriously address the poverty situation in the region, and to encourage popular participation by the poor in programs intended for their own upliftment. Just as the causes of poverty have a regional character, the solutions to poverty reduction and its eventual eradication must be regional. To move forward, SADC must adopt a more proactive and concerted anti-poverty program to guarantee equitable access by all its inhabitants to the region's vast resources.

CHAPTER TWO:
BASIC NEEDS AND DEVELOPMENT

Development entails improving the human condition, combating poverty, and empowering the populace through the provision of basic human needs including adequate food, shelter, clean water, educational, health-care, and employment opportunities. "Absolute poverty," observed then World Bank president, Robert McNamara over two decades ago, "is a condition of life so limited by malnutrition, illiteracy, disease, squalid surroundings, high infant mortality and low life expectancy as to be beneath any reasonable definition of human decency."[1] That powerful reality of absolute social deprivation still haunts millions of our region's inhabitants.

Critical to Southern Africa's well-being is public policy that addresses more decisively the multidimensional conditions of poverty. To be effective, poverty alleviation programs should begin to be synchronized at the regional level. This analysis will review the dimensions of poverty in the region and the intrinsic linkage between basic needs and human development.

DIMENSIONS OF POVERTY

The structures of poverty in Southern Africa vary widely from country to country and even within each country. Poverty is predominant among the rural population, characterized by low life expectancy and high adult illiteracy and infant mortality rates, as well as limited access to basic social services especially educational, health-care, and employment opportunities. In many countries, food security is also still precarious. With the exception of the island nation of Mauritius, much of the region is still severely underdeveloped in virtually every significant aspect of human development.[2]

Poverty in the region has a particularly strong rural dimension. More than 70 percent of the inhabitants still live in rural areas and earn their livelihood directly from subsistence farming. Malawi and Lesotho, for instance, stand out as being the most rural countries, with 86 percent and 76 percent of their respective populations in rural areas.

Rural people bear a disproportionately heavy burden of poverty compared with their urban counterparts. They have much higher rates of under- and unemployment; they lack access to basic services including basic education, primary health care and, in some instances, even to productive assets including land. Land reforms that have been the burning issues, especially in Zimbabwe, South Africa, and Namibia, still lag far behind the people's aspirations and requirements for survival.[3] Thus landlessness among millions of peasants has had a direct link to rural poverty. Although islands of wealth exist in a few urban centers—Johannesburg, Capetown, Harare, Gaborone, Lusaka, and others—the vast sea of the region still lies desolate, unproductive, and largely neglected.

Poverty also has a strong employment dimension. Unemployment in the region, especially among the youth aged eighteen to twenty-four years, has been as high as 40 to 60 percent in countries with little or no safety nets. Thus, the unemployed are among the poorest. There are also millions of others who have been forced into poverty by ill-health, disability, and lack of skills. These are large pools of people rendered unproductive and who have become a social burden. Moreover, the plight of the veterans of the liberation struggle particularly in South Africa, Zimbabwe, and Namibia falls squarely into this category.

Poverty has gender and age dimensions as well. Women, the elderly, and children have been overwhelmed by absolute poverty and squalor, whether residing in rural or urban areas. Also women, whether employed or unemployed, urban or rural, constitute the vast majority of those living below the poverty line, mainly as a result of the inherent gender discrimination in access to economic and social opportunities. The conditions of rural women in particular are further exacerbated by the general absence of basic services in rural areas and their sheer remoteness from the centers of political power, economic activity, and decision making (chapter 4). The elderly and infirm, regardless of their gender, form among the hardest-hit social groups by the conditions of abject poverty. At the moment, only a few countries in the region have attempted to establish viable social security systems or safety nets to protect the elderly, apart from their traditional family support. Also, because of their feeble physical condition, they are unemployable and thus find it difficult to break the circle of poverty.

Thus, a combination of poverty and armed conflicts has had a devastating impact on the region's children. Children under sixteen have fallen victim to the worst forms of malnutrition and lack of access to basic education, primary health care, and decent shelter. Over the past decades, millions of children have perished from preventable diseases, conflicts, and violence. Thousands have served as child soldiers in Angola and Mozambique, thereby increasing their exposure to the trauma of massive violence. Studies by UNICEF have demonstrated that many children, especially those who became permanently incapacitated, were condemned as adults to suffer the lasting effects of poverty.[4]

Basic Needs and Human Development

The provision of basic human needs is critical to the improvement of the human condition. Of immediate importance to the region should be the introduction of universal access to basic education, adequate food, decent housing, primary health care, clean water, and adequate sanitation for all, as well as the creation of employment opportunities. Increasingly, democratization of the political and social institutions has become tantamount to full civil society participation and promotion of partnerships in the fight against poverty and for social justice.[5]

Food security is vital in a region where many countries lack the capacity to feed themselves or to achieve food self-sufficiency for a host of reasons. Among the causes of food insecurity include the land tenure systems that fail to promote adequate agricultural production, especially among peasant farmers; visionless leadership that pursues biased public policy against agriculture in the areas of input provision, marketing, and pricing; fast reduction of arable land and harvested areas as a result of population pressures or hostile environmental factors, including drought and floods; and the lack of food-importing capacity to mitigate hunger. The last factor is primarily the result of many countries being overburdened by external debt and lacking in foreign exchange for any import requirements. Thus, the establishment of standards for food consumption and distribution to ensure adequate nutrition must be given a regional priority.

The fulfillment of universal education, basic health care, adequate clean water, and decent housing promotes a healthy society. Given the severity of rural poverty, these should be among the first steps to reaching the poor and improving their condition. Only a healthy population with minimum levels of literacy would effectively contribute to sustainable development and take advantage of the opportunities so created by economic growth or democratic transformations taking place in the region.

Employment creation is both urgent and critical in every country—from South Africa to Zimbabwe to Zambia, Angola, Malawi, Lesotho and Mozambique—because of the rapid increase in the youth, especially school leavers who must be absorbed productively into the economic system. Moreover, countries such as South Africa, Zimbabwe, and Namibia still very much contend with massive unemployment of war veterans as the direct consequence of the liberation struggles. In many instances, employment creation also needs to be supplemented by the creation of safety nets or income transfers to assist destitute communities and those social groups afflicted with exceptional hardships. Failure to do so has led to the soaring crime rates and mounting discontent likely to result in social instability.

In the final analysis, combating poverty demands good governance and official accountability, without which political strife and high-level corruption only exacerbate conditions of social deprivation. The emphasis in the region should remain on democratic restructuring and reforms to develop both a culture of accountability and full involvement of the poor in the design and implementation of policies that affect their own well-being. This must also entail the poor having direct participation in political decision making and sharing in the economic opportunities of the country. Thus, societies need to mobilize and ensure that poverty alleviation and reduction as well as equitable development become the centerpiece of public policy. This is a particularly daunting challenge for countries like South Africa and Namibia, emerging from highly stratified socioeconomic structures of apartheid.

Human development progress in Southern Africa must increasingly entail the widening of the people's choices and opportunities. However, measured against the complex international standards, the region still lags far behind in many respects. The actual human development or deprivation in any society can be roughly measured through a complex formula of a human development index (HDI), developed by UNDP as a composite index derived from per capita gross national product

(GNP; or a decent standard of living), life expectancy (or longevity), and educational attainment (or knowledge). The HDI values range from 0 (for the least developed) to a maximum of 1 (for the most developed). Countries with HDI values of 0.800 and above are considered to be of high human development level, while those with values between 0.500 and 0.799 are classified as having a medium human development, and countries with values below 0.500 fall under the low human development category or may be classified as poor.

As applied to the region, these measurements show that, with the exception only of Mauritius whose HDI is 0.831 and therefore belongs to a high human development bracket, the rest of the counties are of low to medium human development level (see Table 5.1). Countries with HDI in the medium human development group include Botswana, Namibia, South Africa, Swaziland, and Zimbabwe. However, Zimbabwe has seen a rather dramatic downward slide into extreme poverty in recent years. The other six—Angola, Lesotho, Malawi, Mozambique, Tanzania, and Zambia—are in the low human development category, implying that they are severely underdeveloped or their populations are afflicted with mass poverty. With respect to South Africa and Namibia, however, their statistics tend to be distorted by strong racial biases as a consequence of data that historically excluded the black majority population from opportunities.

The rapid spread of the HIV/AIDS epidemic in the region has also created a new level of impoverishment that has diminished life expectancy in many countries. It has shattered lives and created a new underclass of families victimized by social discrimination on account of their health condition, as well as a preponderance of orphaned children incapable of escaping from poverty.

Conclusion

Absolute poverty in Southern Africa is a condition of so much want, despair, and hopelessness by those who cannot afford even the basic necessities of life. Progressive policies to alleviate, reduce, and eradicate poverty should be measured by the fulfillment of the people's access to those basic human needs including food, health care, education, housing, clean drinking water, and economic opportunities. In doing so, it is critical to democratize the decision-making process, to empower civil society (and especially grassroots support organizations) to promote full participation by the poor in the design and execution of policy.

Poverty eradication cannot be achieved by the government acting singularly or by the people alone without a concerted policy support. It is a partnership endeavor. Government policy must facilitate and, ultimately, its impact should be measured by the extent to which it brings about relief in the quantitative and qualitative improvements in people's living standards and quality of life.

CHAPTER THREE:
Peace, Poverty, and Development

For the past three decades, peace has been elusive in Southern Africa. Countries such as Zambia and Tanzania, although not directly liberated through armed struggle, were adversely impacted because of their firm support for the liberation movements. Traditionally, peace has implied the absence of armed conflict, that is, peace being deemed in terms of the military capacity of a society to wage war or to defend itself against the predatory ambitions of another. That conventional, narrow militaristic view of peace, however, has only limited application. Presently, the main causes of social instability and threats to human security in the region are non-military internal disputes over governance, or the consequences of poverty, hunger, disease, and disparities in the distribution of resources including land.

Threats to Peace

Southern Africa has experienced unparalleled armed conflicts against colonialism and apartheid carried out by the national liberation movements in Angola, Mozambique, Namibia, South Africa, and Zimbabwe. Peace was also threatened throughout the region during the 1980s, as apartheid South Africa lashed out in a destabilization campaign against its neighbors supporting the liberation struggles. It invaded southern Angola in efforts to suppress the ANC and SWAPO forces. It carried out indirect armed aggression by sponsoring, supplying, and logistically supporting the Mozambique National Resistance (RENAMO) dissidents in neighboring Mozambique and UNITA in Angola. Finally, apartheid South Africa also conducted direct military operations against the ANC freedom-fighter sanctuaries in virtually every neighboring country, primarily in Zambia, Lesotho, and Swaziland, and in the newly independent Zimbabwe.[1]

Those military incursions precipitated extreme human insecurity in the region and caused much devastation to infrastructure and severe disruption to the population. Those conflicts also had the effect of depressing agricultural production among the rural populations, which were either displaced internally or forced to become refugees elsewhere. The resultant food insecurity exacerbated the conditions of poverty, hunger, and malnutrition that have continued to plague the region to the present day.

NEW PARADIGMS OF PEACE

With the demise of colonialism and apartheid, the region at the moment enjoys relative peace. But it is also evident that peace is more than just the absence of wars or open conflicts. For peace and human security to endure in the post-conflict Southern Africa, it will be necessary to embrace new paradigms of coexistence, including the removal of potential sources of social instability. Among the dangerous threats to social stability are extreme poverty and social inequalities, disputes over governance, population explosion, mass migration, food insecurity, the spread and stigma of HIV/AIDS, environmental hazards, and personal insecurity resulting from rising crime rates and drug abuse.[2]

Absolute poverty and social inequalities have generated intense debate and disillusionment in the new South Africa, a country emerging from the shadow of apartheid and where the burning land issue remains unsettled. If former president Nelson Mandela's dream and the country's constitutional promises of basic freedom from want, hunger, deprivation, ignorance, oppression and fear, and equal access to land, housing, health care, education, nutrition, and others go unfulfilled, there are ominous signs in South Africa of rising crime and intolerance leading to gross social insecurity.[3] Poverty has already been the source of political instability in the region, as demonstrated by the 1997 coup d'état attempt in Zambia, street demonstrations against escalating food prices, and the recent commercial farm invasions by the landless poor in Zimbabwe.

Movement toward inclusive, power-sharing, and democratic forms of governance enhances peace. It was the circumvention of democracy and promotion of exclusive governance that led to the civil strife in Angola, Mozambique, and apartheid South Africa. Consequently, those governments became more preoccupied with strengthening the military establishment than with improving the human well-being. This was demonstrated by the high ratios of national expenditure on the military compared to amounts devoted to social programs of 30:1 and 20:1 for Angola and Mozambique, respectively, at the peak of the wars in the mid-1980s.[4]

Countries such as Malawi and Mozambique have also experienced explosive population growth with annual rates averaging about 3.5 percent. Consequently, population growth of this magnitude has far outstripped the countries' economic capacities to sustain food security or expand employment opportunities. Meanwhile, the region as a whole has undergone an extraordinary transformation in population migration. Although migrant labor has somewhat tapered down due to rising unemployment in virtually every state and more stringent labor laws, migrations from disasters such as droughts and floods as well as those from poverty-stricken rural areas to towns are on the rise. Also of particular increase have been the opportunistic migrants headed to South Africa attracted by crime, drugs, and better economic incentives than those prevailing in their respective countries. As always, conflicts occur when xenophobia comes face to face with immigrant pressures setting off other forms of discrimination that destabilize relations between citizens and new immigrants.

The lack of food security or presence of chronic hunger has always tormented Southern Africa and been a source of considerable instability. Food insecurity arose as a result of persistent droughts leading to severe shortages in food production that in turn precipitated inhibitive prices for food and essential requirements of the population. Other than South Africa and Zimbabwe, most countries of the region have experienced severe food deficits because of the devastating effects of drought and floods, and their lack of capacity to import food.

The HIV/AIDS epidemic has ravaged the region, and rural women have particularly suffered devastating consequences due to the lack of education and health-care support services. As a result, life expectancy in Botswana, Zimbabwe, and Zambia has declined by 10 to 20 percent. These societies are losing teachers, lawyers, doctors, and government administrators at rates faster than they can be replaced. Hence the epidemic has impacted negatively on their economies as well. The preponderance of orphans in countries devastated by HIV/AIDS has increased the social burden to care for them in societies with few social safety nets.

Environmental damage has emerged as yet another threat to peace in the region. The destruction has emanated largely from three factors: drought, deforestation due to overcrowding or land pressure, and the encroachment of desertification in parts of Namibia, Botswana, and South Africa. Land pressure is especially acute for Lesotho and those areas that once constituted the so-called *buntustan* homelands, including Transkei, QwaQwa, Lebowa, and Ciskei, under apartheid South Africa. In general, as Southern Africa is predominantly rural, environmental damage has impacted adversely on most peasant farmers of the region. It has resulted in the depression of their crop output and heightened food insecurity, as well as caused drastic declines in sales incomes, so much so that large numbers of rural populations have increasingly slipped into more severe conditions of poverty. This has also meant the drift of male labor to towns in search of employment opportunities. Peace has been very much put at risk among the peasant farmers and the indigenous societies such as the Khoi San, who still inhabit the ecologically most fragile areas of the region.

Personal security and safety have been compromised under continuing situations of conflicts, war, physical abuse, torture, and killings of innocent civilians. The frenzies of ethnic-nationalism often get out of hand, as the extreme case of Rwanda warns us. Therefore, there is no denying that a militarized, undemocratic national setting where violence, political intolerance, and crime go unchecked—an environment of anarchy—often begets gross human rights abuses. That is why the first victims of the conflicts in Angola, Mozambique, and now the DRC have been women, children, the elderly, and the infirm. Personal security is further threatened or severely compromised by the self-destructive tendencies of abuse, illegal trafficking, and trading in narcotic drugs that also disproportionately injure the poor in society. Increasingly, illegal drugs have invaded the region and become among the most corrosive threats to personal security confronting the urban centers of South Africa, Zambia, Zimbabwe, and elsewhere.

Conclusion

Peace reinforces development; conversely, conflicts, poverty, crime, and other vices undermine it. Increasingly in Southern Africa, peace can no longer be viewed in the narrow context of armed conflict. Peace now must entail the removal of all potential threats to social stability; foremost among them are the conditions of mass poverty and gross inequalities in the distribution of resources, including land. Peace exists in social restoration of the people's rights to land and resources once denied by colonial neglect and excesses of apartheid. If these are not addressed promptly, conflicts and social strife will destabilize the region, and the struggle between the few haves and the vast majority have-nots to gain access to the basic requirements of survival could elevate into nasty class warfare. At the moment, far too few people have too much, and too many still have too little for survival. Increased crime, violence, protests, and alcohol and drug abuse are among the direct consequences of that imbalance.

The region's economies have collapsed under the heavy weight of conflicts. Many more could crumble further under the heavy burden of poverty. More importantly, conflicts have denied the countries the opportunity to plan, establish development priorities, and fashion coherent public policies to reduce poverty and promote social development. In this regard, the role of political leadership, commitment, and will to stem the escalating spiral of poverty cannot be overemphasized.

CHAPTER FOUR

Poverty and Special Problems Affecting Rural Women

This analysis is probably guilty of attempting to narrow an otherwise broad gender issue. All women in Southern Africa confront unique problems of discrimination and deprivation compared with their male counterparts. In more traditional societies, those difficulties are more accentuated than in countries where modern democratic transformation is taking root. However, virtually no country in the region can claim to have taken the decisive policy measures required to guarantee women's, let alone rural women's, full participation in the development process.

The two UN regional forums on poverty convened in Namibia and South Africa brought into sharper focus the fact that rural women carried a heavier burden of poverty than most in their daily lives. These women were particularly vulnerable to unique forms of discrimination, deprivation, and even domestic violence that warranted special public interventions.

Gender Issues

The region as a whole fares poorly in gender matters. We know that the greater the size of the population that participates in the production of national wealth, the more equitable the distribution of that wealth should be. That has remained a theoretical proposition in Southern Africa. Even in societies where women constitute some 52 to 54 percent of the population and disproportionately carry the burden of agricultural production, they are subjected to income inequalities and overwhelming poverty as a result of underlying discriminatory social structures. While technological advances have resulted in the accumulation of more and more wealth and power by men, women still lag far behind in virtually every important social indicator.

Women have been subjected to mass unemployment, excessive domestic violence, widespread discrimination, and exclusion from full participation in the political and economic agendas of their nations. Of late, they have become disproportionately victimized by the HIV/AIDS disease. In short, women have remained powerless to influence events intended to uplift their own status, and that kind of powerlessness is even more pronounced among rural women.

Over the past two decades, world conferences, combined with women's social activism, have greatly enhanced international awareness about social justice and the status of women—especially with regard to their access to political and economic power, maternal health, education and protection of the girl-child, as well as to their invaluable link to national development. Thus, the challenges of gender balance and the integration of women in development have come to the fore in the international community. The 1985 World Conference on Women, held in Nairobi, Kenya, was among the first to define more concretely gender issues and formulate far-reaching strategies for the advancement of women in all spheres of human development, including the political, economic, and social fields. The 1993 World Conference on Human

Rights, which took place in Vienna, Austria, injected for the first time human rights requirements in gender issues. These included the rights to equal access to basic social needs including education and health care; to equal opportunities for participation in political, economic, and decision-making processes; to equal reward for equal work performed; to equal protection under the law; and to equal rights of all citizens relating to employment, workplace, public, private and even home. The conference also called for the elimination of all forms of gender-based discrimination and stipulated that violence against women was a violation of their human rights. The 1994 International Conference on Population and Development, held in Cairo, Egypt, elaborated the main developmental issues relating to women, including the questions of social access to reproductive health and the protection of the girl-child. The 1995 World Summit for Social Development, held in Copenhagen, Denmark, more vigorously highlighted the parameters of absolute poverty and deprivation among women. It specifically called for greater resource allocation to combat poverty, especially among the most vulnerable social groups—women, children, and the elderly. For the first time, that conference also established time-bound targets and timetables for reducing human poverty through increased access to proper nutrition, education, health care, clean water, adequate shelter, and other necessities of a quality life. Finally, the landmark 1995 Fourth World Conference on Women, held in Beijing, China, adopted the Beijing Declaration and Platform for Action that set forth the long-term and most comprehensive guidelines aimed at removing obstacles to women's full and equal participation in all spheres of public and private life and national development.

All countries of Southern Africa participated in those endeavors. Collectively, those global efforts established three primary objectives by which to measure progress with respect to gender. They were anchored, first, in the promotion of *equality* (actually to achieve full gender parity) and not only *equity* (only to promote social justice) of opportunities for women in society. Second, the conferences sought to ensure the sustainability of such opportunities, that is, to build a lasting foundation for the equal treatment and integration of women in every sphere of social life. And, finally, they highlighted the invaluable link of women's empowerment and gender balance to national development and social progress. Empowerment of women implies full female participation and partnership in the political, economic, and decision-making structures, as well as in their ability to develop the required skills and social connections, which their male counterparts have.

GENDER DEVELOPMENT IN SOUTHERN AFRICA

Southern Africa as a whole has performed poorly in the area of gender-related progress. Of the 146 countries for which the UNDP constructed the gender-related development index (GDI) and ranked them in the descending order of their GDI values (as a statistical measure of progress toward gender equality) in 2000, the majority of the SADC countries were ranked in the hundreds with very low GDI values. The only two exceptions were Mauritius (ranked 59) and South Africa (88) as summarized in Table 4.1 below.[1]

TABLE 4.1:
Gender-Related Development Index for SADC Countries (Year 2000)

Countries	HDI rank	GDI value	GDI rank
Angola	161	N/A	N/A
Botswana	126	0.566	104
Lesotho	132	0.521	111
Malawi	163	0.389	137
Mauritius	67	0.762	59
Mozambique	170	0.307	144
Namibia	122	0.604	101
South Africa	107	0.689	88
Swaziland	125	0.567	103
Tanzania	151	0.436	126
Zambia	153	0.424	129
Zimbabwe	128	0.545	107

Source: UNDP, *Human Development Report, 2002* (New York, OUP, 2002), Table 1, pp. 149–152; Table 22, pp. 223–225.

Notes: HDI—human development index—is calculated by UNDP as a proximate measure of a country's human development or social progress level based on international statistics of life expectancy at birth, adult literacy, access to education or knowledge, and GDP per capita (reflective purchasing power parity rates of exchange).

GDI—gender-related development index—applies the same factors as in HDI above, but adjusted for gender disparity.

Since South Africa began its post-apartheid democratic transformation in 1994, it has moved rather boldly and decisively on the gender front. Women in South Africa hold more significant elective and decision-making positions in major institutions, including parliament, university, central bank, and the courts, than elsewhere in the region. Gender balance in decision making should be viewed as more than just the appointment of women to the cabinet. To become national players, women need to occupy high-profile positions of influence in important statutory institutions such as Speaker of parliament, governor of the Central Bank, chancellor of the University, chief justice of the Supreme Court, and similar areas of prominence in the private sector. In that respect, countries such as Zambia, Tanzania, Zimbabwe, and Botswana, in spite of their long periods of stability, still lag far behind and have a considerable distance to traverse before measuring up to this critical area of human development. The experience in South Africa is also reflective of the work of vibrant NGOs and women's lobby organizations and networks. It is thus encouraging to observe the mushrooming of women-based NGOs and other groups throughout the region. They should now begin to compel more progressive public policy interventions relating to poverty eradication and gender balance.

SPECIAL PROBLEMS AFFECTING RURAL WOMEN

Among all vulnerable social groups, rural women bear the brunt of poverty. Female-headed rural households invariably live in absolute poverty. Lesotho illustrates this phenomenon succinctly. Although statistics suggest that three quarters of households in Lesotho are male-headed, 75 percent of rural households are effectively female-headed due to excessive male labor migration to South Africa. Thus agricultural work is left primarily to women and children, while, at the same time, women seldom have full access to critical assets including land, capital, and rural inputs required for successful production.

Rural women experience the highest unemployment and underemployment with rates ranging from 60 to 90 percent. These unemployment statistics are three to four times the depression levels of any economy. They also serve as both farm- and domestic workers for commercial farmers and related employers, particularly in South Africa, Namibia, and Zimbabwe, and therefore fall victim to landlessness and poverty level wages. As non-unionized labor, they are not in a bargaining position for liveable wages or for demanding improvement in their working or living conditions. The level of domestic violence inflicted on rural women that goes unreported is staggering. There are inadequate policing or communication systems in rural areas through which to report incidents of violence. Rural women, like rural people generally, are subjected to discrimination with regard to access to social services and budgetary resource allocation, especially with respect to educational and health-care services. Hence illiteracy and maternity-related deaths have been on the increase.

Following a short spell of the euphoria after independence in the 1960s, the deepening economic crisis of the 1970s and 1980s hit hardest at the rural poor. The external debt crisis, in particular, has diminished the capacities of countries of the region to make social investment, resulting in almost complete collapse in rural infrastructure. The World Bank and IMF structural adjustment programs as applied in Malawi, Mozambique, Zambia, and Zimbabwe have inflicted devastating human casualties in rural communities, particularly among women and children.

For Malawi and Mozambique, rapid population growth has also far outstripped their capacities to produce food, create employment, and expand the required social services including education and health care. For rural women, rapid population increase implies more mouths to feed. Hence, they have had to work longer hours to search for food, fetch water, and care for children. Civil conflicts and natural disasters that have ravaged the region have taken their toll on rural women particularly in Angola and Mozambique, resulting in the depression of food production and leading to widespread hunger, malnutrition, disease, and death.

Traditionalism in countries like Lesotho and Swaziland also imposes discriminatory, minority status on women. It limits women's access to land, credit, and social participation and has had a profoundly detrimental effect on rural development. Related to this is the growing disintegration of the family throughout the region as a result of divorce and desertion of men, who migrate for better opportunities elsewhere. As these migrant workers find new partners, single motherhood and female-headed households increase in their countries of origin, and so too does abject poverty.

Public policy has been deficient in addressing the challenges of rural poverty. Policy deemed as being anti-poor and anti-rural hampers development in general and impacts more negatively on the welfare of rural women in particular. I suggest that three factors do motivate public investment directed to rural areas. First, it is driven by the ideological stance to spread development benefits to all corners of the country, as was attempted by Tanzania soon after independence. Second, there is the need to gain political support of the rural electorate, and finally it is motivated by the desire to augment public revenue by broadening the national tax base.

Political considerations have been paramount thus far in resource allocation policies by the countries of the region. Tanzania, for instance, in its early stages of post-independence socialism, vigorously pursued a combined politically and ideologically driven program to spread the benefits of modernization to the rural people.[2] In recent times, the political imperatives to combat the pernicious inequalities inherited from apartheid have compelled South Africa to advocate more aggressive rural investment measures. The secondary motivation for the rural policy in South Africa is that of land reform intended obviously to bring about a measure of social justice to the victims of land dispossession under apartheid and, by so doing, to guarantee continued rural support for the ruling ANC. On the other hand, in typically rural countries such as Malawi and Mozambique, where public investment is likely to bring about an increased peasant market production, a huge potential exists for a significant expansion of the tax base. In countries with greater dependence on the urban industrial sector, notably Zambia and Zimbabwe, public resource allocations tend to be biased toward urban areas, often to the detriment of the peasant-dominated rural sector. Moreover, rural population including rural women does not display much political activism and organizational clout comparable to the unionized urban-industrial labor. All other things being equal, government tends to direct public investments to the more politically organized and vocal urban sector. Thus, some of the poverty typologies that were identified by studies elsewhere do have application to varying degrees in Southern Africa as well.[3]

Rural women are among the poorest and most deprived in the important areas of education, health care, decent housing, adequate nutrition, and social security, as well as in the consumption of durables. When asked what she understood about poverty, a woman in Langa township, South Africa, once said "It is being isolated, not having food, living in a crowded home, not having water and lights and the lack of secure work and income."[4] Rural women thus find themselves to be isolated politically and physically from the centers of power and economic opportunity. Like any marginalized social group, they feel alienated by the seemingly exploitative structures of the state they do not fully comprehend. Their very dependence on husbands or male partners for survival tends to reinforce the feeling of inferiority and hopelessness and to deprive them of the ability to bargain for power independently. As a result, in spite of their numbers, their capability to coalesce effectively, to influence progressive agendas in their favor, remains negligible. Today, rural women are still far from gaining access to decision-making powers that even their urban counterparts have begun to acquire. In many instances, educational limitations continue to constrain their ascendance to elective offices or to heading major institutions in society.

To counter these overwhelming negatives, it is imperative for the regional leadership to reform the political, social, and cultural structures that inhibit women's progress and to mainstream rural areas, and rural women in particular, in the national development programs; to redirect increased social investment to education, health care, creation of small-scale credit and provision of agricultural services, promotion and expansion of employment opportunities, social security, human rights and personal protections affecting rural women. Therefore, improving the welfare of rural women is a challenge that all societies throughout the region must embrace; it is a challenge as compelling as that of eradicating extreme poverty itself.

CONCLUSION

Southern Africa still lags far behind in addressing the critical challenges of gender balance and gender development, especially the plight of rural women. Although a few individual countries seem to be moving more aggressively, many have hardly begun to deal with this crucial policy matter. No state in the region can claim success in attempting to reach the internationally required parity of women's empowerment and their participation in decision-making and national development programs, including poverty reduction and alleviation strategies.

With women constituting the majority populations in some countries, the lack of progress in this critical area will continue to constrain development and undermine the goals of social justice. Public policy must foster more aggressively practical ways to integrate women in development beyond the mere rhetorical platitudes that have characterized the debate thus far. Policy should be measured by concrete outcomes—by the expanded opportunities for all citizens, by ensuring increased access to gainful employment, education, health care, proper nutrition, clean water, and other social services—as the starting point to improving the human condition. These efforts will remain elusive unless countries concerned and the region as a whole start to define and set firm targets and timetables for rural women's improvement and education of the female children. Clear targets should also be adopted to enhance women's involvement in government, statutory bodies, institutions of higher learning, and the private sector. Gender reforms should not be held back the same way that land reforms have dragged on for ten or twenty years. Doing so would be tantamount to undermining any form of national democratic transformation and, therefore, of social progress. Thus, public policy should encourage the formation of women's grassroots organizations and networking in town and country to engender broader participation and input by voters in national development interventions. Governments in mature democratic societies by and large do respond to the voices of organized electorate.

CHAPTER FIVE:
POVERTY AND PUBLIC POLICY
— COUNTRY PERSPECTIVES

The human faces of poverty in Southern Africa include women, especially rural women, the unemployed, children, the elderly, and domestic, farm- and migrant workers, as well as the internally displaced population and refugees. To these, add the indigenous communities including the Koi and San people who inhabit the remote settlements of the Kalahari in Botswana, Namibia, and South Africa. The severity of poverty and deprivation among these groups differs widely from country to country, and so do policy interventions intended to alleviate their plight. One thing is common though: policy interventions have largely failed as poverty has escalated and equitable development remained elusive.

THE POLICY DETERMINANTS

Public policy is very much a function of the political environment in which it is exercised. Southern Africa has gone through various political upheavals that have shaped some of the current development policies. They include (1) patterns of social mobilization against colonialism, (2) effects of the armed struggle for national liberation in Angola, Mozambique, Zimbabwe, Namibia, and South Africa, and (3) impact of civil wars that ravaged the post-independence period in Angola and Mozambique.

With a few exceptions, the more peaceful the transfer of power, the more moderate the nationalist transformation agenda became. Conversely, those countries that waged long and bitter armed struggles became more radicalized and less accommodating to the vestiges of colonial development. The very peacefully negotiated decolonization of Lesotho (1966) and Swaziland (1968), for instance, left intact the monarchy structures and other social contradictions that discourage equitable development and impact adversely on the poor, especially with regard to gender balance. Rural women in Lesotho and Swaziland still lack access to the critically important productive assets of land and credit due to their so-called minority status; that is, they are legally treated as underage people unable to own property or enter into contractual obligations.

Meanwhile, the independence of Tanzania (1961) and Zambia (1964), although achieved peacefully, ushered in more militant and activist political and economic agendas and transformation programs, but to different ends. Tanzania pursued a vigorous socialist path in the early period of independence to fight poverty and strengthen rural development.[1] In the post-Nyerere period, however, that socialist agenda has been abandoned for a pragmatic market approach. In Zambia, with a dominant mining-urban industrial complex, the government pursued a nationalization program of the productive assets with an urban bias, while largely neglecting rural development. At the same time, the country lacked the managerial skills required to coordinate an efficient modern economic management. That contradiction between the need to expand ownership and the capacity to manage it resulted in the collapse of the once vibrant economy and caused the Zambian people to slide into abject poverty. On the other hand, the current Zambian policy of embracing unfettered privatization and liberalization to placate the

World Bank and IMF has only exacerbated the conditions of poverty. Today, its social services, including education and health care, have collapsed, unemployment has escalated, and hunger, extreme poverty, and deprivation have become increasingly harsh and more pernicious.

Malawi was another example of the region's disastrous experiments. Following its independence in 1964, Malawi was saddled by Kamuzu Banda's autocratic regime, which lasted well into 1990s. For three decades the country was subjected to one of Africa's gross misrules and heavy-handed statism that skewed development policies in favor of a few ruling elites and militated against the poor. As a result, Malawi also created and nurtured a culture of dependence that undermined development and social progress.

The advent of independence in Angola and Mozambique (1975), Zimbabwe (1980), and Namibia (1990) initially brought a welcome relief from the human suffering of the past decades. That respite, however, was short lived as Angola and Mozambique were immediately plunged into civil wars precipitated by disputes over governance and sheer greed for power. Insurgent rebellions armed and logistically supported by apartheid South Africa wreaked havoc in both states, effectively tying up resources in military activities away from any social investment. That resulted in the widespread conditions of absolute poverty and squalor that have continued to characterize both countries.

Zimbabwe and Namibia, although initially pursued more aggressive agendas of reconstruction and development, were bogged down by severe constitutional restrictions and protections for minority populations that owned and controlled virtually all arable land and commerce. To dislodge them from their positions of privilege and to effect meaningful reforms in favor of the black majority has been virtually impossible. Land redistribution to the landless peasants has been stifled by the exorbitantly priced buyout schemes that states could not afford. Thus, much-awaited land reforms in Namibia and Zimbabwe have effectively stalled, resulting in the desperate landless poor, in the case of Zimbabwe, having to resort to invasions of white-owned farms with very negative development consequences.

The 1990s brought much promise. Autocratic, one-party regimes in Malawi and Zambia crumbled and gave way to more democratic governance. In 1992, peace returned to Mozambique. And finally, in 1994, apartheid in South Africa was dismantled and replaced by a democratically elected government, and peace began to return to the entire region. These events sparked a new impetus for more and concerted regional renewal. At the country level, social reconstruction would entail the restoration of the shattered economies, people's basic rights to land and property, and reunification and rehabilitation of families long split by conflicts and apartheid. And at the regional level, renewal would include rebuilding of infrastructure of common interest to restore collective institutions in order to promote confidence among SADC countries as they move toward integration.

POVERTY-REDUCTION AGENDAS

Applying the policy constructs outlined above, countries of the region have pursued vigorously pro-poor, or anti-poor, neutral, or hardly any discernible policy regime at all as far as poverty eradication is concerned. Pro-poor agendas have entailed those reinforced by state policy instruments such as the constitution, annual budgets, or other documents intended to rally national consensus for anti-poverty programs. For post-apartheid South Africa, and to some extent in Namibia and Tanzania, government policy on poverty has been guided by the profoundly progressive pro-poor constitutional provisions as well as by the ideological stance. In South Africa, the people's rights to basic needs, including housing, health care, and education, were elevated by the new constitution to almost equal status as the right to citizenship. It established statutory commissions for human rights and gender issues to monitor compliance. The government has published or caused the publication of policy reports intended to highlight and make the poverty agenda the policy centerpiece for equitable development. More critically, the poverty-eradication agenda of South Africa has been championed by the same vibrant civil society organizations, the apartheid-era battle-scarred labor movements and NGOs, that now serve as the uncompromising vanguards of the cause of distributive justice in the society. In Namibia, the constitution mandated compulsory primary education for all, although it was not explicit on other equally critical basic social requirements. However, because of its size, Namibia still lacks the civil society structures strong enough to monitor effective state compliance in the fulfillment of social investments. In Tanzania, as already pointed out, poverty alleviation was ideologically driven by the country's socialist agenda in the early years of independence. As such, budgetary allocations, public mobilization, and the overall national policy trust were focused on rural development and poverty reduction. Although a reorientation of that policy has recently been undertaken, poverty reduction has continued to be the uppermost focus in Tanzania to avoid social fracturing.

The second set of public policies are those perceived to be anti-poor in that they tend to promote structures of social neglect, especially with regard to rural areas. By and large, colonial and apartheid South African policies followed that pattern of benign neglect of rural development. In recent times, some constitutional provisions that constrained public policy in Zimbabwe, South Africa, and Namibia from meaningful intervention to achieve equitable land and wealth redistribution have the same effect of being anti-poor; they inhibit rapid national transformation to improve the welfare of the majority populations. The compensation requirements in favor of the current landowners have hampered any progressive land reforms from being implemented in Zimbabwe and Namibia. However, unlike the other two countries, South Africa has the capacity to mobilize the funds required to carry out the necessary land reforms, although the huge amounts envisaged to buy out a few farm owners would draw substantial resources from other critically deserving social investments in education, health care, and other services.

Countries like Botswana, Malawi, and Zambia have pursued somewhat neutral poverty-reduction policies; that is, while not promoting anti-poor programs per se, they have not, at the same time, devised credible poverty-eradication strategies. On the other hand, Angola and Mozambique have been preoccupied militarily since independence such that they were by and large unable to devise meaningful policies of fighting poverty and achieving equitable development. The two states have continued to be marred by conflicts and matters of state survival. In addition to internal difficulties, other external factors including drought, floods, external debt, HIV/AIDS, and other diseases have been equally debilitating to the region.

COUNTRY PERSPECTIVES:
THE POVERTY POLICY PARAMETERS

Policies to reduce poverty have varied widely from country to country in Southern Africa.[2] Table 5.1 summarizes some of the socioeconomic indicators of poverty by the countries concerned. When assessed against the HDI (a UNDP-established index as a proximate measure of the level of human development and social progress), out of 173 countries included in the study in 2000, all SADC countries, except Mauritius (which ranked 67th), ranked in the hundreds. Meanwhile, seven of these countries—Mauritius, South Africa (ranked 107), Namibia (122), Swaziland (125), Botswana (126), Zimbabwe (128), and Lesotho (132)—fell in the medium development category. The other five—Tanzania (151), Zambia (153), Angola (161), Malawi (163), and Mozambique (170)—were ranked in the low development group. Extreme poverty and underdevelopment throughout the SADC region are characterized by a very high proportion of rural population still largely dependent for its daily livelihood on subsistence farming, by low life expectancy, high adult illiteracy and infant mortality rates, as well as by low levels of access to education, health care, proper nutrition, safe water, and other basic requirements of life.

Angola and Mozambique, for instance, although occupying opposite ends of the subcontinent, share substantial commonalities in social formations inherited from their Portuguese colonial experience. The two Portuguese-speaking countries in an overwhelmingly English-speaking region have also been constrained by language from fully articulating their development requirements and benefiting from meaningful resource sharing. More important, development in both countries has been inhibited by prolonged and debilitating conflicts that began as anti-colonial wars and subsequently turned into decades of equally bitter civil wars. As a consequence, both countries have continued to suffer from severe poverty conditions.[3]

In many respects, Angola and Mozambique are not inherently poor. Angola is a well-endowed country with vast mineral wealth, the world's richest diamond deposits, and off-shore oil reserves. Other mineral resources in Angola include quartz, iron, copper, manganese, gold, and zinc. As primarily an agricultural country, Mozambique, on the other hand, possesses more modest resources. However, it has a highly developed hydroelectric energy sector, with the Cabora Bassa scheme as its centerpiece, and is potentially capable of supplying power to the entire Southern Africa. Both countries are still predominantly rural with 65 percent of Angola's and 68 percent of Mozambique's populations residing in rural areas and engaging primarily in subsistence farming.

Post-independence Mozambique and Angola lacked peace for an extended period of time. Mozambique became embroiled in a civil war with the RENAMO soon after its independence in 1975 until their 1992 peace accord. Angola also fought a bitter bush war with UNITA from the time of its independence in 1975 until 2002. In addition, the two countries were victimized throughout the 1980s by acts of aggression and destabilization by apartheid South Africa. They also suffered disproportionately from the impacts of massive displacements of the population, famine, and severe scarcity of skilled labor to carry out development.

Table 5.1:
Southern Africa: Social/Poverty Indicators

	HDI rank (2000)	Total population Million (1996 - 2000)	Rural population % of total (1995- 2000)	GDP per capita US$ (1995 – 1997)	Life expectancy Years (1995 – 2000)	Adult illiteracy % (1995 - 2000)	Infant mortality rate (Per 1000 live births) 1995	Population per doctor (1990 -1997)	Daily calories Supply per capita (1992)	Access to safe water % of population (1990-1998)	Human development index (HDI) 1994
Angola	161	13.1	65	410	44.6	63.0	172	25,000	1840	32	0.335
Botswana	126	1.59	60	3020	44.42	23.8	74	4,162	2280	70	0.673
Lesotho	132	2.1	76	770	51.2	17.6	92	20,000	2201	57	0.457
Malawi	163	11.3	86	170	40.7	40.9	125	45,000	1827	54	0.320
Mauritius	67	1.2	59	3380	70.7	15.5	17	1,300	2696	100	0.831
Mozambique	170	18.3	68	80	44.3	56.0	115	33,000	1680	28	0.281
Namibia	122	1.8	69	2000	45.1	35.5	62	4,200	2120	57	0.570
South Africa	107	40.0	45	3160	56.7	33.0	55	1,700	2705	70	0.716
Swaziland	125	0.94	64	1170	50.8	21.1	101	6, 600	2706	---	0.582
Tanzania	151	35.1	68	120	52.1	25.9	104	25,000	2021	69	0.357
Zambia	153	10.4	55	400	40.5	23.0	112	14,000	1931	47	0.369
Zimbabwe	128	12.6	65	540	42.9	13.0	73	7,500	1989	74	0.513

Sources: UNDP, *Human Development Report 1997* (New York: UNDP/
Oxford University Press, 1997), various tables on profiles and trends
in development; A. A. Lighelm, *The Southern African Development
Community* (SADC) (Pretoria: University of South Africa, 1997); UNDP,
Human Development Report 2002 (New York, OUP, 2002), Table 1
(pp. 150–152), Table 5 (pp. 163–165), Table 6 (pp. 167–169).

Poverty in Angola and Mozambique manifests itself in very low life expectancy of only forty-four years and among the highest infant mortality rates in the region with 172 and 115 deaths per 1,000 live births, respectively. Health-care infrastructure in the two countries also collapsed following prolonged periods of armed conflicts. The doctor to patient ratios of 1:25,000 and 1:33,000, respectively, are among the worst in the world. Similarly, malnourishment is rampant, especially among women and children emerging from their refugee life. This is illustrated in part by the very low calorie (energy) consumption among the adult populations in these countries of 1,840 and 1,680 calories, respectively, per person per day. More importantly, especially for children, has been the lack of access to safe water. Only 32 percent of Angolans and 28 percent of Mozambicans had access to potable water between 1990 and 1998, resulting in a disastrous impact on health as manifested in high child mortality statistics.

Over the past decades, Angola and Mozambique have been unable to develop viable policy interventions to reduce poverty. For its part, Angola has never left the transitional stage of a war-torn economy to a period of rehabilitation and reconstruction, notwithstanding the end of military hostilities in 2002. In 1993, the government launched a national reconstruction plan externally funded by the World Bank that, in reality, turned out to be a post-war rehabilitation effort. It focused in part on debt relief as well as the cost of peace efforts, including demobilization of soldiers, de-mining, providing assistance to returning refugees, rehabilitation of the displaced population, and conduct of the elections. No economic or social infrastructure reconstruction was actually undertaken. Food security in Angola has also remained precarious as more than one half of its food requirements are imported. The population survives largely on external assistance, mostly from Western aid donors and UN organizations.

The picture for Mozambique, however, brightened after the 1992 peace accord that ended the conflict with RENAMO. The 1994 multiparty elections also democratically legitimized the government of President Joaquim Chissano to undertake bold measures of economic restoration. Although policies to combat poverty are still haphazard, the focus is mainly in the areas of land reform, human capital investment, disaster relief measures, and institutional rebuilding.[4]

Land reform for Mozambique has implied land liberalization by putting more land into the hands of both small and commercial farmers, moving away from the existing land ownership structure that vests all land in the state. In 1996, Mozambique and South Africa agreed to set aside large tracts of land in the northern part of the country to be leased to South African commercial farmers as a means of boosting food production. Foreign donors also provided US$200 million in assistance to Mozambique, conditional on promotion of peasant access to arable land and stable land rights.

Human capital investment and the rebuilding of the country's social infrastructure, including basic education, primary health care, and nutritional services, as well as ensuring access to safe water and adequate sanitation have became paramount in Mozambique. Rudimentary social safety nets have been restricted mainly to supporting drought and disaster relief victims, with food and nutritional assistance to 3 million displaced people as well as support for pregnant women, malnourished children, the aged, handicapped, and female-headed households. Institutional restructuring has been initiated as a poverty-eradication measure. By 1994, for example, poverty alleviation units were beginning to be established to strengthen the design, evaluation, and monitoring of poverty-reduction efforts nationwide. On the whole, however, Mozambique still lacks a credible and coherent anti-poverty program.

Poverty in Botswana is primarily a rural phenomenon and most severe among the country's 60 percent rural population.[5] On the other hand, only 29 percent of the urban population falls into the poverty category. Geographically, rural poverty is concentrated and especially severe in the western part of the Kalahari. Nationally, 50 percent of female-headed households in Botswana experience greater conditions of poverty when compared with 44 percent among male-headed households.

The main causes of poverty among the Batswana people include unemployment, poor wages for those who work, a narrow economic base around urban diamond mining, inequitable distribution of income, lack of skills among the people, hostile semi-desert climate, drought, and poor soils. The importance of cattle-raising also impacts Botswana's poverty levels among the rural population. Some 300 large-scale commercial farmers who own approximately one fifth of the national total herd of cattle dominate the cattle industry. As for small farmers, the economic benefits of beef exports only accrue to some 50 percent of the households that own an estimated one half of the country's cattle herd. The other 50 percent of the rural households that neither own nor have access to cattle are therefore among the most poverty-stricken population.

Botswana has taken considerable strides to improve people's access to basic services, although the quality and spatial distribution of those services are still somewhat inadequate. The distribution of educational services is still largely skewed against the rural and remote areas of the country. As a result, children in rural areas lack equitable access to basic education, health care, clean water, and other essential services, and therefore still contend with absolute poverty.[6]

These deficiencies notwithstanding, Botswana made remarkable progress on several fronts during the 1990s. Life expectancy rose to the global level of sixty-five, only to plummet to forty-four years in recent years, mainly as a result of the impact of HIV/AIDS that infects nearly a third of its population. However, in other important areas, including adult literacy and infant mortality rates that continue to torment many of its neighbors, Botswana has continued to make progress. More important, nutritional standards in Botswana have remained among the highest in the region, with daily food intake of 2,280 calories per adult person per day, exceeding even internationally recommended levels.

Although not pursuing a directly pro-poor activist agenda, Botswana's impressive development performance can be attributed largely to its stable political environment. The smooth changeovers in political leadership have ensured policy continuity and consistency in the development sphere. In addition, Botswana has also had a stable economy that has attracted and retained external investment even during the darkest periods of the liberation struggles of the 1970s and 1980s.

The severity and structure of poverty in the tiny mountainous Kingdom of Lesotho is quite unique.[7] Here poverty has very strong rural and gender biases. An estimated 76 percent of the country's population is rural and suffers from an acute shortage of fertile land as the country lacks any known resources except, as the saying goes, its "people, scenery and water." The vast majority of Lesotho's rural population consists of women engaged in agricultural activities; 25 percent of the male labor has migrated to work in the South African urban-industrial complex.

Lesotho's extreme poverty is thus the consequence of the lack of resources and economic opportunities, including employment and a productive rural sector. Poverty manifests itself in the struggling rural women attempting to work tiny, uneconomical smallholdings under conditions exacerbated by drought and environmental degradation.

A comprehensive Sechaba study of 1994 classified Lesotho's poverty-stricken population into two main categories: the poor and the very poor.[8] The study concluded that while the unemployed, migrant, domestic, and those working for poverty wages fell into the first category, the second group consisted predominantly of women and children. The analysis found that while in 1986 an earning equivalent to US$6 per person per month (or 20 cents per day) constituted the minimum wage for human survival in Lesotho, by 1996 that amount had risen to US$8. In other words, anybody earning less than US$8 per month in 1996 was below the country's survival or poverty line. As a result, some 65 percent of Lesotho's population had slipped into extreme poverty, with the vast majority of them earning less than poverty wages. The number of the very poor households has also increased in the capital town of Maseru as elsewhere in the country. The study further found that poverty was also exacerbated by the fact that some 20 percent of the rural Basotho people were landless, and 47 percent of the farmers did not own livestock, a very important store of wealth in that society.

Clearly, extreme poverty in Lesotho falls disproportionately on female-headed households and those without wage earners. By 1996, households without adult wageworkers had increased to 22 percent in Maseru and 65 percent in rural areas where the vast majority of female-headed households were without wage earners. The problems of poverty and unemployment were worsened by the retrenchment of the Basotho migrant workers from the South African mines, the persistent drought, and the high inflation the economy was experiencing at that time.[9] In summary, extreme poverty in Lesotho is the result of a multitude of factors, including the people's lack of access to adequate clean water, good roads, wage employment, primary health care, adequate sanitation, and the lack of ownership of the critical assets of land and livestock.

Policy intervention to alleviate and reduce poverty has not been vigorous. Foremost among the major constraints has been the instability in the country's governance. Lesotho's political scene has for a long time been one of considerable turmoil, a struggle between the royal family and the governing elites. At one point, the army also had a stake in governance. As the case of Botswana demonstrates, political stability breeds economic progress and a more focused policy and continuity in pursuit of social development. More recently, Lesotho experienced turmoil involving the royal family, government, and the army. An external military intervention force led by SADC (South Africa and Botswana) was called in to restore order. The rebellion and riots it precipitated resulted in much destruction and, in effect, an exacerbation of poverty in the country.

The traditional land tenure has also marginalized women in a country where they carry a disproportionate burden of production. It severely undermines not only poverty initiatives but the larger social development goal as well. Although a strong NGO community, including the Lesotho National Council of Women and the umbrella Lesotho Council of NGOs, is now emerging to prod and monitor social development and gender progress, more fundamentally, legislative and policy interventions are required to institute meaningful land reforms, strengthen gender equality, and expand women's access to credit and other opportunities. For Lesotho, which is characterized by a heavy male-migrant labor phenomenon, women form the backbone of the local economy, and improvement in their welfare is critical to national progress.

Finally, Lesotho lacks resources with which to pursue bolder and more aggressive pro-poor policies. While the Highland Water Project is beginning to bear fruit by generating capital for development, the magnitude of poverty is simply colossal. The government, therefore, will have to forge stronger partnerships with NGOs, other SADC partners, and international development agencies to make a greater impact on the country's poverty alleviation efforts.

Malawi is a predominantly rural country with 86 to 90 percent of its population earning a living directly from subsistence agriculture.[10] In virtually every sphere, Malawi has a severely underdeveloped economy, characterized by serious socioeconomic deficits. Its life expectancy of forty years is comparable only with that of Zambia, two of the lowest in the region. The country has a severely underdeveloped health infrastructure with a ratio of one doctor to 45,000 people, and an infant mortality rate of 125 per 1000 live births, some of the worst statistics in the region. A host of factors contribute to Malawi's extreme poverty and deprivation. These include low agricultural output and productivity, limited employment opportunities, low levels of education, inadequate social infrastructure, lack of safety nets, low nutritional levels leading to generally poor health among the population, limited credit services (especially for smallholder farmers), low non-farm wages, rapid population growth, environmental degradation, and limited access to productive land.

The human development crisis in Malawi, as indeed throughout the region, has also been exacerbated by the spread of the HIV/AIDS pandemic. AIDS has not only continued to reduce life expectancy, but also impacted negatively on the country's productivity through its effect on labor and the increased social dependence ratio, the number of orphaned children to support compared with the economically productive adults in the household to care for them. The country has lacked a vigorous or coherent poverty-eradication policy to deal with these concerns. For three decades, the policy placed the state at the center of development; it set both the pace and managed the stage for all actors in development. That highly centralized power in the hands of a few ruling elites viewed the people as mere tools or passive recipients of development and not the principal actors. It thus demoralized them and inhibited popular participation in the political and economic processes of the country.[11] That is what the present-day Malawi is struggling to turn around.

In terms of public policy, Malawi has never fully developed an anti-poverty agenda. In the waning period of the autocratic rule of Kamuzu Banda, the international community sanctioned the country by freezing assistance in order to increase pressure for political reform. While that political strategy worked, it also worsened the conditions of poverty in the country. Following the election of 1994, the new government of Malawi still lacked the capacity—human, financial, and technical resources—to roll back the old statism. The new Bakili Muluzi government has the task of empowering the poor to enable them to address the challenges of their own survival. It also still lacks institutional structures for policy design and implementation concerning poverty. Therefore, three fundamental challenges face today's

Malawi: the first is the compelling urgency to tackle the structures of mass poverty, unemployment, and other ills among its population; second is for the government to develop strong partnerships with civil society organizations so as to capacitate them to effectively address the enormous poverty burden and human suffering confronting the country; and third, to increase the literacy level of the people with a bias toward women and rural areas. Organizationally, the media, NGOs and other grassroots institutions in Malawi need to monitor closely the implementation of poverty-reduction programs to ensure that the new government remains focused on development and does not fall into the old pattern of excessive resource misallocation.

Despite its abundant natural wealth and commendable strides toward development, Namibia is still afflicted by grinding poverty, especially among its rural population.[12] Fifty-two percent of Namibians survive below the poverty line. The country is still predominantly rural, with 69 percent of the people residing in the countryside, largely in the northern regions, and engaged in subsistence farming. Seventy percent of rural Namibians are poor.

Namibia, however, continues to register considerable progress in other fields, including education that was constitutionally mandated and health care that has resulted in substantial reductions in infant mortality rates from over 100 deaths per 1,000 live births at the time of independence ten years ago, to the current level of 62 per 1000.[13] The illiteracy rate has also continued to decline markedly since 1990, and people's access to other basic needs has increased. However, like other countries of the region, the ravages of HIV/AIDS have rapidly eroded Namibia's health gains.

The country thus faces mounting challenges including (1) the urgent need to reduce poverty that still ravages the vast majority of its inhabitants; (2) the compelling need for land redistribution to the landless poor; (3) the urgent desire to reduce unemployment, especially among the youth and war veterans, as well as to mitigate glaring income and wealth inequalities; and (4) the critical importance of developing the capacity to husband scarce water resources in a partially desert country.

Poverty among rural Namibians is largely the result of the people's lack of access to adequate land. Sixty percent of the country's prime land is still in the hands of a small white population, just as approximately 2,000 white commercial farmers who raise cattle and sheep and produce other products dominate the country's agriculture. On the other hand, land hunger afflicts hundreds of thousands of rural families in the northern and southern regions. Land hunger reduces the peasant farmers' capacity to produce adequate food for their own subsistence. Land reform has been extremely slow in Namibia; it is one of the country's most failed policy areas and likely to spark social instability.

Land acquisition and resettlement programs have been constrained by inadequate legal and financial mechanisms for their implementation. Given these factors, it is unlikely that the recently projected target of getting 80 percent of the land to the country's landless poor would soon materialize.

With approximately 55 percent of Namibia's population below the age of twenty, the country is under pressure to expand employment opportunities for the youth and the jobless ex-combatants. The unemployed are among the poorest, and to combat poverty, the country needs to expand job-creation programs in both urban and rural areas. There is a distinct potential for the development of agro-industrial activities in the northern region. With no employment generation, poverty will increase, and the income and opportunity disparities in the country will widen and continue to be a source of disharmony. The country's income and wealth inequalities currently rival only those of South Africa and Brazil.[14] The World Bank has estimated that the 7,000 richest Namibians (consisting of less than 0.5 percent of the population) command the purchasing power equivalent to that of the country's 800,000 poorest people, or 50 percent of the population.

Those extreme poverty and income disparities are obviously an invitation to social conflict and instability.

Finally, as a semi-arid country, Namibia needs to carefully husband its water resources to support the chronically drought-stricken rural population. This has already compelled the country to engage in joint water conservation ventures with its SADC neighbors.

Development in South Africa represents a complex juxtaposition of extreme material wealth amid abject poverty, deprivation, and politico-social exclusion as the last vestiges of the apartheid era. The real change in South Africa today, therefore, is not that the victims of apartheid are suddenly better off, for they are not. The true change lies in the fact that the freedom won in 1994 unleashed a new energy, an intense debate about the country's future, and a genuine desire by South Africans to find enduring solutions to the underlying conditions of extreme poverty and inequalities. South Africans are attempting to reinvent their country, to start all over again!

In August 1997, the country's civil society, in collaboration with UNDP and other UN agencies, declared war on poverty, stressing that in the post-apartheid era, the most important priorities and greatest challenges were poverty eradication and redressing inequalities. "We dedicate ourselves to concrete actions and real commitment to create a world in which humankind can live in peace and justice, and to declare war on poverty and inequality that it may be eradicated from our land" the declaration concluded.[15] The government of South Africa subsequently endorsed that declaration as a framework for popular mobilization to combat human poverty and deprivation.

For South Africa the struggle is far from over. After going through three and a half centuries of struggle for political freedom and social justice, and nearly half a century of the struggle against the doctrine of apartheid, the struggle for economic and social justice has now begun in earnest. Expectations and aspirations of the poor were raised to phenomenal levels by the demise of apartheid and introduction of the new political and constitutional order. The country's new constitution entrenched the fundamental socioeconomic rights long denied the population under apartheid, including the rights to adequate housing, basic health care, education, nutrition, clean water, and the right to family and parental care for young children, among others.[16] The constitution also put in place powerful statutory safeguards, principally the human rights as well as the gender equality commissions to monitor national performance and compliance with respect to those commitments. That is why, in a land with such a fundamental commitment to human dignity, there was uproar in 1997 when a kidney patient, Thiagraj Sobramoney, was left to die because he was too poor to afford a transplant.[17]

Poverty and inequality throughout South Africa manifest themselves in high rates of unemployment, extreme land hunger, and lack of access by the overwhelming majority of the population to basic human requirements as guaranteed by the country's new constitution. In both urban and rural areas, the country's majority population is confronted with blight, severe deprivation, and squalor.[18]

Statistical evidence is quite startling. Fifty-three percent of all South Africans live in absolute poverty, and the country's adult illiteracy rate is 65 percent. Strong racial, geographical, gender, and age dimensions characterize endemic poverty. Ninety-five percent of South Africa's poor are black Africans; 75 percent of them reside in rural areas, especially in those provinces that incorporated the former homelands primarily in the Eastern Cape, Kwazulu/Natal, and Northern provinces. Nearly 87 percent of the land, a crucial asset for the rural people, is in the hands of the minority whites that account for only 10 percent of the population. Thus 90 percent of the South African people occupy only 13 percent of the national territory. Unemployment among the youth aged eighteen to twenty-four runs as high as 40 percent. Joblessness has been further aggravated by the demobilization of soldiers from the former armies that fought against each other during the apartheid period.[19]

Women, children, the elderly, and the disabled in South Africa bear the brunt of poverty. Female-headed households, for example, have a 50 percent higher poverty rate than those headed by males. Sixty-one percent of all children live in poverty; for black children, it is more than 70 percent living in poverty. An estimated 2 million to 3 million South Africans are malnourished, including 87 percent of black children under the age of twelve. As a result, more than 45 percent of all the poor in South Africa are children under the age of sixteen. Between 40 and 50 percent of the absolute poor households comprise those out of the labor market, the elderly and people with illness or disabilities (including crippled miners) who depend on pensions and remittances as the primary sources of livelihood. The poor who work earn less than one tenth of the country's richer top 20 percent of the households.[20]

The spatial concentration of poverty in South Africa is equally alarming. More than two thirds of the poor are found in three of the nine poorest rural provinces with the Eastern Cape and Northern Province having by far the highest poverty concentrations of 78 percent and 77 percent, respectively. The level of abject poverty in these provinces and Kwazulu/Natal is closely linked to their incorporation of the ten poverty-stricken, squalid former homelands created during apartheid. Of those former homelands, Transkei, Qwa-Qwa, and Lebowa were the poorest reserves of cheap labor during apartheid, with poverty rates respectively of 92 percent, 88 percent, and 83 percent, respectively. The vast majority of the poor in these areas are women and children left behind by urban male migrant workers.[21]

By 1997, in terms of HDI, South Africa was basically a poor country that ranked 90th out of 175 countries, trailing behind Chile, Malaysia, Mauritius, Brazil, and Algeria, among others. However, the human development levels for white South Africans were higher, comparing favorably with more developed, middle-income countries like Cyprus and Barbados. For black South Africans only, the country's human development levels fell to 125th, a position below those of Botswana, Indonesia, Egypt, and Swaziland, among others.[22]

So where does the new democratic South Africa start from in responding to these challenges? South Africa cannot afford to do nothing or move gradually without damaging its social image. The country is thus preoccupied with the twin challenges of alleviating poverty and achieving equitable development. It has tackled both issues principally through the application of three policy instruments: first, through the constitutional provisions that entrench basic human needs as being fundamental human rights requirements as well; second, through the launch in 1995 of the Reconstruction and Development Programme (RDP); and finally, through the Growth, Employment and Redistribution: A Macro-Economic Strategy (GEAR) adopted in 1996. RDP was a more radical and down-to-earth strategy for social renewal in the post-apartheid transformation than GEAR. Its aims were principally to democratize the state, rebuild the country's peace and security structures, and begin to attack the conditions of extreme poverty and unemployment, and to redress the gross inequalities in the society. RDP had focused primarily on programs to meet the basic needs of South Africans, including expanding the investment in education, health care, and housing, as well as in the development of human resources and skills, among others.

It was a major setback for the most needy South Africans when RDP was suddenly abandoned and replaced before its full implementation by GEAR in 1996. The GEAR strategy, on the other hand, while significant and forward-looking, tends to moderate RDP's more immediate and people-centered goals. In practical terms, GEAR's focus is on the rebuilding and restructuring of the economy to meet long-term challenges of creating employment and redistributing incomes and opportunities, while ensuring universal service delivery and the creation of social safety nets. Thus, that program has somehow lost the immediate transformational imperatives for social justice that RDP was designed to address. Since its launch, however, there has been an increased social activism by civil society organizations to refocus national energies on the issues of poverty and social upliftment. In October 1996, the national parliament conducted a snap debate exclusively to highlight poverty within the framework of the 1995 World Summit for Social Development. By October 1997, and as part of the observance of the International Day for the Eradication of Poverty, the country engaged in a nationwide debate on poverty eradication in provincial legislatures, workshops, and other outreach activities to promote increased awareness about the conditions of poverty and the efforts under way to address them. Throughout 1998, national poverty hearings were conducted by civil society organizations to highlight widespread pain and anguish among the desperately poor in both urban and rural South Africa emerging from its apartheid past.

South Africa today faces extraordinary challenges. It still has a long distance to traverse on the transformation front, but the vision and will are emerging and resources exist to tackle the vexing issues at hand. Poverty in South Africa is not just about the income poor but also about the people's lost creativity and potential to contribute to society that must now be rekindled. It is about the denial of access to opportunities and choices for so long to lead decent lives, achieve a better standard of living, more freedom, dignity, and self-respect—things that matter most for human existence.

Swaziland's development experience is somewhat atypical in the region. Poverty is not as extensive as it is in its neighboring countries. Although 64 percent of the country's population is still rural, only 45 percent are considered to be poor.[23]

The other human development indicators for Swaziland are also mainly favorable. The country's life expectancy of fifty-one years is also among the highest by Southern African standards. Even the deteriorating infant mortality level of 101 per 1,000 live births is still modest when compared with the extreme statistics of Angola and neighboring Malawi and Mozambique. Meanwhile, some 60 percent of Swaziland's population has access to clean water, and the adult literacy rate of 79 percent is also among the highest in Africa.

However, of late, the main challenges facing Swaziland include the devastating impact of HIV/AIDS, which affects nearly 33 percent of its adult population; rigid traditional structures that constrain equitable development; and inadequate institutional reforms intended to bring about greater gender parity in the society. The role of a dominant monarchy in Swaziland has its social cultural advantages but serious developmental limitations as well. On the one hand, the monarchy appears to enhance social cohesion through a form of cultural affinity or commitment, especially among the rural population that rallies around it as the unifying symbol for social progress. On the other hand, it inhibits the development of modern political and social formations, freedoms, and participation essential to accelerating the overall economic upliftment of the society. In view of this, the country's labor movement and other civil society organizations have recently been agitating for the return to multiparty politics banned since 1973. Thus, the traditional structures of Swaziland constrain development by their failure to promote popular participation by all citizens in the political and economic life of the state.

As a result, social reforms in Swaziland need to include the improvement in the legal status of women. Sixty percent of Swaziland's population, the vast majority of it women, is engaged in subsistence agriculture. With agriculture the country's mainstay, the importance of the role of women cannot be overemphasized. It is therefore imperative for them to gain greater access to productive assets including adequate land and credit services. At the same time, land tenure and agricultural activity on the Swazi National Land would need improvement to enhance the country's overall productive capacity.

Tanzania more than any other country in the region, embarked on a bold socialist transformation program to address the country's widespread poverty shortly after gaining its independence. With a vast majority of its population rural and poor, the Nyerere government's ideological goal was to build an egalitarian society directed at improving the welfare of the peasants, the backbone of the country's economy.

The 1967 Arusha Declaration envisaged development through socialist self-reliance to synchronize poverty alleviation around three tenets: (1) an interventionist agenda that aggressively pursued nationalization of the country's strategic private enterprises; (2) rural development through a village regrouping program; and (3) a stubborn resistance to external dictates of the World Bank, IMF, or other lending institutions.

Rural development through villagization or *Ujamaa Vijijini* became the cornerstone of poverty reduction. By 1977, some 13 million Tanzanians were related or belonged to 8,000 villages. The program made remarkable achievements in service delivery, especially in the area of universal primary education, and instilled in Tanzanians a sense of common national identity. At the same time, however, the socialist program had drawbacks in that it required far more resource input than the state could possibly mobilize. As a consequence, it dampened the overall economic performance of the country.[24]

That period of social activism concluded, in large part, with the retirement of its architect, the late former president Julius Nyerere in 1985. Since then, development in Tanzania has taken a more pragmatic market-oriented approach. At present, Tanzania is still 68 percent rural and poor, with a life expectancy of fifty-two years and an infant mortality level as high as 104 per 1,000 live births. The current policy challenges relating to poverty reduction have taken on a dual approach of rebuilding the requisite institutions geared to private management of the economy, as well as of providing greater support for poverty-reduction endeavors by focusing resources to selected priority sectors including basic education and primary health care.

The national strategy has aimed at promoting alliances or partnerships between government and civil society organizations as well as working with the poor themselves to mobilize resources for the eradication of absolute poverty by 2010. The strategy rests on three components: capacity-building for the poor, creating an enabling environment for combating poverty, and identifying and promoting selected priority sectors.[25]

Capacity-building and social empowerment have gone hand-in-hand by focusing on employment creation to raise income levels among the poor as well as the promotion of cooperative structures in both agricultural and industrial sectors. An enabling environment for poverty reduction, however, has emphasized the promotion of good governance, abolition of official corruption, and establishment of poverty-alleviation organizational networks consisting of the government, the poor, and civil society. Critical in this area has been the promotion of full participation among various stakeholders in the design and implementation of anti-poverty programs.

The priority sectors identified include those likely to exert maximum human impact in the shortest possible time. They focus on the promotion of primary and technical education, strengthening health services, enhancing clean water supply and sanitation services, improving food security requirements, promoting private sector investment in industrial development, emphasizing job creation in small-scale mining, and protecting the environment.[26] These are measures that have also found support from the World Bank, IMF, and other leading donor communities and partners.

The extremely severe poverty levels confronting Zambia are a recent phenomenon, beginning in the 1980s. Zambia is not inherently a poor country but has been impoverished by the destructive policies of the past decades. Since independence, the country has gone from a middle-income, vibrant economy to one of the least developed countries or the poorest of the poor in the world. Today, Zambia's levels of poverty and underdevelopment in the region rival only those of once war-torn Angola, Mozambique, or DRC.

Two factors have accounted for Zambia's rapid slide into extreme poverty: first, it served as the center for the prolonged wars to liberate Southern Africa that sapped much of its vast resources; second, it was a victim of gross economic mismanagement characterized by one-partyism throughout the 1970s and 1980s that destroyed the economy and people's faith in themselves. The return to multiparty democracy and the coming into power of MMD in 1991 subjected Zambia to massive deindustrialization in the name of pursuing economic liberalization, which we now know, was accompanied by ruthless official plunder of its national wealth. While the support for the liberation struggle was a noble cause to free Southern Africa, the structures of a one-party state as well as the massive closures of companies and economic plunders of the 1990s were destructive to Zambia's development capacity.

By late 1980s, poverty had struck hard at the country's population, especially among the disabled, the aged, the orphans and neglected children, female-headed households, and the homeless. Eighty percent of Zambia's rural households, 26 percent of those in urban areas, and 60 percent countrywide became either poor or severely poverty-stricken by 1989.[27] That picture only worsened during the 1990s, as a series of surveys by the country's Central Statistics Office found that, by 1991, about 61 percent of all Zambians were absolutely poor, 10 percent moderately poor, and 29 percent were not poor. Those statistics dramatically deteriorated by 1996, as poverty levels and people's suffering escalated to alarming proportions with 80 to 90 percent of Zambians facing a constant struggle to survive.[28]

Regrettably, the above served only to demonstrate that the democratization that began in 1991 did not bring with it much developmental impact. Instead, as a result of unfettered economic liberalization, companies were closed, throwing thousands of workers on the streets. Unemployment soared, and extreme poverty and hunger afflicted the lives of millions of Zambians on a daily basis. Education, health care, and vital agricultural services also collapsed, thereby debilitating the country's overall development. The standard of living of most Zambians is at present worse than it was at the time of independence four decades ago. Extreme poverty among Zambians manifests itself in the escalation of unemployment, especially among the youths, widespread malnutrition, homelessness, abandoned street children, general ill-health, and collapsed education and health-care infrastructure. The social groups most severely impacted by poverty are the destitute, the disabled, the elderly, children (especially those orphaned by the HIV/AIDS pandemic), women (more particularly single, female-headed households), and the homeless. As this human tragedy unfolded, the country's life expectancy has declined dramatically from fifty-four in the late 1980s to thirty-seven years at present. Although Zambia is one of the most urbanized in Africa, its infant mortality level of 112 per 1,000 live births is also among the highest in the region, a reflection of its poor health care as well as nutritional deficiencies.

Zambia thus faces monumental policy challenges including an urgent need (1) to reduce human poverty, especially in the neglected rural areas, (2) to create employment opportunities to absorb an increasing number of young job seekers, (3) to enhance social empowerment in national development and governance, especially among women by ensuring their participation in decision making, (4) to promote agricultural production and increase productivity, particularly among small-scale farmers as a means of spreading equitable development, combating poverty and hunger, and improving nutrition, (5) to strengthen the contribution of civil society in dealing with social issues and matters of national governance, and (6) to institute social safety nets intended to mitigate the severity of absolute poverty among the most vulnerable Zambians.

Unfortunately, Zambia today still does not have a national plan to attack poverty and address these concerns in any sustained fashion.[29] Strategies to reduce poverty have also been bogged down by blind, unfettered pursuit of privatization. Urgent poverty-reduction measures should be initiated at four levels: the first should be to stop the human suffering while holding the line on everything else. Employment, education, health care, and improving agriculture and the nutritional level should be given top priority. All of these would require direct public investment beyond just privatization. Public investment targeted to public works would create employment opportunities while, at the same time, rebuilding the country's shattered economic infrastructure. Private investment should be encouraged and channeled toward rejuvenating the country's idling industrial capacity, especially in those sectors likely to support agricultural development and food production. Education requires short-term rehabilitation and long-term expansion, as well as the introduction of universal compulsory schooling until grade 12. This would ensure that educated children would not become the victims of absolute poverty as adults. Education should also entail retraining or upgrading labor skills of workers for modern industrial application, especially those young workers who have lost employment elsewhere. Health care implies enhanced investment to upgrade the current dilapidated, overcrowded, and antiquated facilities. This should ensure the provision of first-rate and decentralized health-care services for women and children. Health-care requirements also need to be integrated with improved nutritional standards and provision of clean water, particularly in the rural areas.

Second, Zambia needs to remedy gender discrimination. As chapter 4 demonstrates, Zambia's gender record is among the worst in the region, and the country has yet to adopt a coherent gender policy. Women still lack access to political power and decision-making structures, hence the overwhelming feminization of poverty. More women need to participate in elective politics and be involved in senior-level decision-making positions of statutory bodies such as the university, central bank, parliament, commissions, and boards. All laws, especially some oppressive customary laws and practices, need to be reformed to promote gender equality and elevate the status of female citizens. In keeping with international covenants and conventions, an enlightened national policy must seek to eliminate all forms of exploitation, abuse, harassment, and violence against women.

Promoting agriculture, food security, and rural development must now take a center stage as a way of poverty reduction, particularly since copper is no longer the economic king in the country. Effective product pricing and marketing policy as well as promotion of agro-industrial development would enhance rural development and job creation. As rural production remains predominantly a female occupation, access to adequate land and credit facilities for women should be paramount as a means of improving their welfare. Rural areas themselves need to be made more physically accessible. Implementation of rural renewal programs are needed to rehabilitate the old and build new infrastructure, including feeder roads capable of supporting an expanded economic modernization program.

Social activism needs to be encouraged and nurtured in combating poverty. Zambia is home to about thirty grassroots NGOs delivering vital community and social services. NGOs, including religious institutions, have increasingly become pivotal stakeholders in poverty-eradication endeavors. Some provide valuable home care for those stricken with HIV/AIDS, others care for the orphans, and yet others deal with empowerment programs such as civic education and vocational training. Public policy should thus attempt to integrate these civil society programs into a coherent national strategy of community partnership, empowerment, and human development. The country is also home to a robust labor movement consisting of miners, teachers, local government workers, and others. They should not be undermined by public policy but reinforced in their quest to improve wages, conditions of service, housing, and other human-impact efforts intended to reduce poverty.

Finally, Zambia needs to develop credible social safety nets or social protections for the needy. The government-operated public welfare assistance scheme is rudimentary and targets only a small proportion of the poor. Over a four-year period between 1992 and 1996, the current public assistance program managed to assist only 840,000 out of some 7 million needy persons including orphans, the disabled, elderly, women, and others.[30] In a country sliding fast into crushing poverty, social safety nets must be expanded and become more inclusive. In these vital areas, public policy needs to forge partnerships with civil society and business communities to mobilize resources and address the complex issues of social security, unemployment protection, disability benefits, medical support costs, nutritional provisioning, and other requirements for the most needy. Critical to any effective implementation of a viable safety net system would be civic education to ensure that all stakeholders know the obligations and benefits such programs would entail. It must be recognized that the greater the involvement of civil society, including labor and business and especially beneficiaries in the development of the program, the deeper the sense of community ownership of those efforts become.

Zimbabwe's rapid degeneration into poverty and pernicious economic crisis is the result mainly of two overriding issues: (1) the almost intractable land distribution imbalance that condemns millions of rural Zimbabweans to abject poverty, and (2) the pervasively statist public policy that includes mismanagement of the economy coupled with rampant official corruption. In the region, Zimbabwe is one of the best-endowed countries with natural and human resources. Indeed, at the time of independence in 1980, Zimbabwe, like neighboring South Africa, enjoyed one of the highest living standards in the world, although most of that wealth was narrowly concentrated in the hands of the white minority community.

Zimbabwe's history is replete with battles fought over land. With 65 percent of the country's population rural, land or the lack of it has been one of the major sources of both wealth and grinding poverty. For the 70,000 whites who own 85 percent of the land, it has brought them much prosperity and boundless comfort. Meanwhile, for the millions of landless families, the lack of access to adequate land has subjected them to a life of perpetual poverty, malnourishment, and squalor. During the colonial time, black inhabitants were thrown off vast tracks of land that were given to white settlers. As a result, today, just 4,500 white commercial farmers occupy more than 70 percent of all prime or arable land in the country. By any conceivable standard, that is a recipe for conflict.[31]

Thus, extreme poverty in Zimbabwe is predominantly a rural phenomenon. Hence, land reform is critically required as a first step to combat poverty and redistribute land to poor peasant families. The question of land was entrenched in the independence constitution by colonial Britain to ensure the protection of hundreds of white-owned farmlands. Land in the country cannot be expropriated from those owners for redistribution without exorbitant compensation and application of the principle of "willing seller, willing buyer." But that is precisely where the catch is; land reform has been stalled in Zimbabwe because there are not many willing sellers among the farmers, nor are there adequate funds with which to acquire the land.

In 1997, the government attempted to grab 1,500 white farms for redistribution. But the white farm owners foiled that effort in the country's courts. Eventually, fifty farms were apparently bought, but even those properties did not reach the needy landless peasants. Instead, the country's ruling leadership has been accused of allocating the acquired prime land to its cronies. Thus poverty continues to ravage the Zimbabwean countryside, and rural families do not have adequate land on which to settle and produce food for the growing population. Consequently, unemployment has risen to as high as 60 percent and malnutrition is widespread. The poverty rate in rural Zimbabwe is 70 percent, especially among women, the young, and veterans of the liberation struggle. These conditions, together with the massive urban joblessness, pose a grave threat to the country's social stability, as was witnessed recently when Harare was rocked by huge protests and strikes over price increases for food, fuel, and other essential commodities.

Mismanagement and corruption have also eroded Zimbabwe's promise.[32] While the country has preached activist development policies, practice has not quite matched the fierce rhetoric. Statist policies that drowned Zambia and Malawi apparently have found a new home in Zimbabwe, where it dampens the people's ingenuity to be creative in order to help themselves. Apart from the abuse of land reforms, the ruling elites have been accused of feathering their nests at the expense of the poor. The country's Legal Forum recently issued a scathing indictment against corrupt practices resulting from centralized power. It noted that bureaucracy and red tape had inhibited the access of ordinary citizens to certain services and compelled them to bribe public officials. Other notable corrupt practices included the looting of the War Victims Compensation fund, abuse of housing schemes, and the continued flouting of the established Tender Board Regulations. The point here is that corruption is detrimental to development and saps investable resources away from such essential services of the country as education, health care, and other basic requirements.

Zimbabwe has not yet developed a cogent poverty-reduction strategy. Recently, however, a community of NGOs has emerged. The essential partnership in combating poverty, involving government and civil society, has also begun to take root, although the business community including commercial farmers remains lukewarm to these initiatives. As regards the NGOs, the African Community Publishing and Development Trust has stood out in its involvement in social mobilization as well as in capacity-building efforts in the rural areas. It has targeted its programs to the remote communities of the country. Similarly, the Organization of Rural

Associations for Progress is also engaged in institutional development through funding of small self-help rural projects. To combat rural poverty, these efforts would require a sustained public policy reinforcement that is still lacking in Zimbabwe.

CONCLUSION

Southern Africa is a land of extreme diversity, contrasts, and great potential. Yet the region faces no greater challenge now than that of creating an environment of peace, of combating extreme poverty, and of promoting more sustainable development. That also entails, among other compelling goals, promoting transparent and accountable governance, embracing pluralism in political and economic spheres, creating wealth and more equitable structures in the distribution of income and such wealth (especially land), eliminating all forms of gender discrimination, and enhancing social partnerships in finding enduring solutions to human problems. That is a tall order.

In country after country, public policy has faltered in addressing the pressing human needs. A UNICEF poster starkly depicts an African child's dilemma when asked the question: "What do you want to be when you grow up?" "Alive," the child responds, underlying the prevailing human tragedy in Southern Africa. Youths are no longer pursuing grand dreams but simply the fulfillment of the fundamental right to life. Public policy has been found wanting and inconsistent in fighting poverty, feeding the hungry, educating the young, or providing the economic opportunities (including employment) required to sustain a decent life. A new form of vitality is now emerging, however, by way of grassroots advocacy organizations including NGOs, churches, peasant farmers, shantytown dwellers, women's groups, indigenous minorities, labor unions, human rights, and others working for peace and improvement in the human condition. They should keep governments' feet to the fire to ensure that policy interventions facilitate and not hinder the tackling of poverty and achievement of social justice. Only that, in the final analysis, would guarantee peace and security, social harmony, and cohesion in the region.

CHAPTER SIX:
POVERTY-ERADICATION IMPERATIVES

Prescription is often hazardous. It is particularly more so for Southern Africa, a region with a web of complexities at the political, social, economic, and cultural levels. Development for the region rests on political leadership honoring its social contracts with the people through good governance, popular participation, and forging partnerships with civil society to alleviate poverty and redress social injustice.

This analysis highlights some of the practical challenges that must be tackled to enhance the regional development and poverty-reduction agenda. These include: (1) creating a political environment that embraces peace as the prerequisite for development, (2) pursuing economic growth with equity, (3) maximizing people's access to resources, including land and social services, (4) promoting empowerment, particularly of women, and their integration into national development, (5) forging sustainable development at the country and regional levels, (6) linking poverty reduction to budgetary allocations, and (7) maximizing the benefits derived from external assistance.

These are obviously mammoth tasks. But they are sufficiently compelling requirements for nation-building and regional development.

The experiences of the UN regional forums on poverty held in Namibia and South Africa demonstrated, if anything, that the weaknesses of public policies lie in their failure to involve the people in the design and execution of programs intended to improve their human condition. While some countries like South Africa command more dynamic and vibrant civil societies to carry out social mobilization for human upliftment, many have remained handicapped and lack political and institutional capacities to tackle poverty.

PEACE AND DEVELOPMENT

Peace and peaceful resolution of conflicts are paramount for the region to achieve security and social progress. While conflicts waged over colonialism and apartheid were justifiable on moral grounds, the fratricidal discords in Angola and Mozambique were not. Those conflicts were primarily the result of political greed and lust for power by a few. Unelected regimes sought to monopolize all power to the exclusion of others, and those in opposition wanted to shoot their way into government. The consequences resulting from that struggle were devastating for ordinary people in the two countries and the entire region.

On the other hand, we have noted that stability reinforces social progress and prosperity. The shining example in our region is Botswana, where it was demonstrated that political stability and discipline enhanced economic expansion. Throughout the 1970s and 1990s, Botswana experienced growth at an average rate of 7.3 percent annually.[1] Although it still had its share of poverty and unemployment, it achieved remarkable prosperity during the darkest periods of the region's political turmoil.[2]

Conflicts in the region have been caused by persistent disputes over governance. Therefore, to avoid future strife or discords, we need to reform the political landscape and governance. Political leadership needs to construct more responsive and accountable forms of governance. To begin with, constitutionally imposed term limits should be respected as representing the will of the people. Where such provisions do not yet exist, they should be instituted to guarantee some measure of predictability in the society; populations should reasonably look forward to an orderly change in leadership. Such transitions enhance stability and continuity, and therefore better promote peace and social progress. The lessons of Nelson Mandela (South Africa) and Ketumile Masire (Botswana) are instructive in this regard.

Second, political discourse should not be about a mere pursuit of power but a civil contest of ideas and contrasting visions. This implies that those with power have an obligation to be magnanimous in the exercise of that power among their people. They need to reinforce the democratic values of fair play, political maturity, inclusiveness, tolerance, and nonviolence in settling political differences. Power and arrogance do not mix. If they do, they pose a grave danger to the nation state and society. Those in opposition should not be branded as the enemies of the state but as fellow compatriots and patriots who happen to view things differently and are intent on restraining the abuse of power. The opposition bears equal responsibility to advance peace and nation-building by being constructive and mission-driven in its advocacy for change and an alternative policy agenda. While political opponents do not necessarily have to agree, they need to guarantee a civil dialogue and debate of ideas.

Third, sources of conflict should be reduced through recourse to and respect for the rule of law. Excessive political arbitrariness breeds disputes. Countries, individually and collectively, must encourage the creation of truly independent judicial bodies and human rights monitoring structures that command the respect and confidence of all. When courts speak, people need to feel that justice has been dispensed fairly and equitably.

Fourth, the region needs to reduce the glaring inequalities in the distribution of wealth and critical resources, including land. Zimbabwe, South Africa, and Namibia are particularly vulnerable in these areas. They are heavily burdened by the most inequitable systems in the distribution of income and wealth. Such development disparities, particularly in land allocations, constitute an immediate threat to peace with serious repercussions for the region. The recent Zimbabwean farm invasions by the poor sound a timely warning about the dangers of allowing extreme injustice to fester.

Finally, and related to the above, is the urgent need to more effectively tackle the region's abject poverty that inflicts so much human suffering. The fact that poverty casts an ominous shadow and could become a major source of civil discord is now a settled debate. We know that war veterans, the unemployed, landless peasants, the poor, and destitute are already wreaking havoc in Zimbabwe, Namibia, and South Africa as they seek to highlight their plight. Clearly, these social groups cannot be expected to remain passive and disciplined forever in the face of the increased adversities they have to endure on a daily basis. They need relief and a stake in their respective societies.

GROWTH WITH EQUITY

Three critical challenges now confront the region: to expand opportunities for all through economic growth; to achieve equitable distribution of development; and, at the same time, to mitigate absolute poverty afflicting its people. They are not inherently incompatible. While growth will be critical to expand the economic pie, public policy must be targeted to compensate for market imperfections in order to promote social justice. In countries such as South Africa, Zimbabwe, and Namibia with deeply fractured ethnic societies, the principle of shared growth as applied in the East Asian experiences could be instructive.[3] In many instances, public policy interventions would bring about not only rapid structural growth but also equitable distribution of the benefits of such growth among the carefully targeted social groups. In the cases of South Africa, Zimbabwe, and Namibia, growth must be in favor of the once-excluded and disadvantaged black majority communities.

How would the concept work? I suggest that it should entail the setting up of clear targets and timetables for narrowing the glaring wealth gaps. As the black population was the most deprived and marginalized under both the colonial and apartheid systems, black South Africans would need accelerated affirmative support to rise beyond their present levels. Policy should clearly stipulate that within a given period of time, say ten years, the black population would manage and own at least 50 percent of all enterprises in the country. Public policy should also determine the desirable employment participation levels that would reflect more accurately the ethnic composition in the society. By a certain period of time, a given percentage of all managerial positions must be occupied by those who had hitherto been excluded. Public policy should dictate timeframes by which to reduce the incidence of poverty from, say, the current levels of 70 percent to a more socially tolerable 50 percent level or below. The global millennium development goals, for instance, have already established timetables and benchmarks of halving poverty by 2015, and the countries concerned should adhere to those targets. Finally, the other critically important programs that need to be instituted to promote shared growth include the provision of universal primary education and enhanced access to secondary and higher education, proactive support for small and medium-size enterprises, and people's increased access to health-care services and other social requirements. Sound development policy strategies should always have a component of social protections addressing the well-being of the most vulnerable in society including children, women, orphans, the elderly, retirees, unemployed, homeless, and others too weak to fend for themselves.

In the case of South Africa, the growth and employment strategies launched in 1996 have fallen short on distributive justice. As a result, while some of these efforts have received instant acclaim from the business sectors, they have tended to alienate civil society organizations including labor and NGOs.[4] If implemented strictly as designed, some of those programs, especially the 1996 growth strategy, could exacerbate rather than narrow the prevailing inequalities in the country, leading to increased social cleavages and instability.

Critical to the success of the shared growth development strategy is the creation of broad-based deliberative bodies of stakeholders to spearhead and monitor its implementation. Civil society and the private sector in particular must be invited to participate in the design and implementation of policies that would be relevant to their respective interests. Such deliberative bodies would also establish resource allocation rules that would be clear to all participants, reassuring them of their mutual benefit from growth and equitable distribution of wealth.[5]

ACCESS TO LAND AND SERVICES

In South Africa, Zimbabwe, and Namibia, where land allocation was severely artificially distorted, agrarian reform is paramount to combat poverty. Land is a burning issue in those countries, because land was more severely concentrated in the hands of only a few white commercial farmers to the exclusion of vast numbers of peasant or smallholder farmers. As a result, land scarcity has caused extensive rural poverty, reduced food security, and contributed to gross unemployment among the rural poor. Thus, the strategy in these countries should be to accelerate land redistribution to the landless peasants and other reforms to enhance rural production, employment creation, and food self-sufficiency. Such reforms, however, also need to be accompanied by more pro-poor, pro-smallholder agricultural policies that enhance peasant farmers' access to credit, inputs, and extension and market services.

Land utilization in the urban areas was equally distorted by colonial and apartheid policies along racial lines. That resulted in urban settlements characterized by extreme dispersion and fragmentation. The location of high-density, low-income areas at the urban fringes—Soweto of Johannesburg, Highfields of Harare, Katutula of Windhoek, Matero and Chilenje of Lusaka—while at the same time concentrating all employment opportunities in the city centers, undermined the efficient functioning of cities as economic units. Furthermore, that state of affairs increased the cost of providing services including transportation, piped water, education, and health care. More critically, it also reduced the productivity of labor as a result of fatigue from long commutes and lack of time for skills development. The agenda for urban restructuring to combat urban poverty is thus just as urgent and imperative as the agrarian reforms necessary to fight rural poverty.

Social Empowerment

Genuine development must entail enhancing the people's capacity to actively participate in influencing social change. This analysis has noted Southern Africa's weak human development capacity despite its abundant natural wealth. The critically missing element has been the people's full participation in the development process. This lack of popular participation initially caused by colonial or apartheid exclusion has been sustained by the dysfunctionality or deficiency of the present governance structures that do not maximize people's involvement. Therefore, empowerment would demand a more aggressive promotion of people's full participation in shaping the critical decisions affecting their lives. It would give priority to the well-being of the most marginalized members of society, especially women. It would demand political and governance structures to be accountable in addressing the issues of social consensus. It would call for the empowerment of women through political and economic emancipation and their involvement at high levels of decision making. It would demand the integration of women into the leadership roles in parliament, cabinet, political parties, and ownership of the major enterprises and means of production. That would also entail that women's education and skills development take a center stage; that legal structures be developed to prohibit gender discrimination in access to land, credit facilities, and other opportunities; and that women's integration as full partners in national development receive national priority. Public policy would need to remain firm on this critical issue and promote not just gender equity but equality—that is, striving toward the realization of equal numbers of women and men in key sectors of national governance.

SUSTAINABLE DEVELOPMENT

Poverty in the region is the result of the people's lack of access to land, credit, skills, employment opportunities, and power, especially access to decision-making structures. Sustainable development must start at the micro or household units and be extrapolated to the national and regional levels. It implies enhancing the people's livelihood, that is, "the ability for people to make a living and improve their quality of life without jeopardizing the livelihood options of others."[6] Implementation of this concept in the region would involve four interrelated elements: community participation in the assessment of social and survival requirements; the analysis of the macro, micro, and sectoral requirements of land, credit, social services, and so on; an establishment of the potential contribution that technological innovations and skills can make to social improvement; and finally, an identification of the social and economic investment required to move the community out of poverty. Efforts under way in Malawi show considerable promise in the integration of household food security, environmental management, and skills development among village entrepreneurs.[7] To reduce the vulnerability of the poor and improve their condition at the regional level will require similarly coordinated programs for SADC to tackle the structures of poverty on the regional scale. SADC should also ensure a targeted programming of poverty-impact assistance in areas such as nutrition, education, health care, clean water supply, proper sanitation, and population and family planning.

Linking Poverty Reduction to National Budgets

Poverty-eradication strategies have significant implications for the allocation of scarce resources. Therefore, it is critically important to "mainstream" poverty into the national budgetary process. Poverty reduction or poverty-impact expenditure must constitute clearly identifiable items under the expenditure plans and departmental budgets. This would, for the first time, provide a yardstick against which to assess or measure the delivery performance by each unit of government of the amount of public expenditure devoted to this crucial area.

Related to this should be four elements to facilitate policy assessment. First, countries in the region need to carry out social audits of policies in the context of their impact on the poor. Second, the countries concerned or donors should develop poverty-impact statements for every national sector. These should contain clearly measurable achievement indicators relating to poverty reduction that should be fulfilled by a given amount of resource commitments. More and more resources should be devoted to reinforcing the sectors with high performance rates in the poverty-impact areas. Third, it is important to provide adequate training for those handling the issues of poverty assessment and analysis at policy and operational levels. That in turn would facilitate proper targeting of budgetary resources and evaluation of the impact of national programs.

The final policy element must be that of creating partnerships and establishing poverty-monitoring bodies.[8] The number of NGOs and related civil society advocacy organizations has mushroomed in the region. These organizations have increasingly taken on the monitoring role of social development. Critical also is the creation of independent statutory bodies to monitor policy performance in the whole spectrum of social upliftment. In South Africa, the Commission for Human Rights has fulfilled that function of assessing poverty-reduction efforts in the context of the fulfillment of human rights as stipulated under the country's constitution. It should be these organizations and institutions, including the media, that must persist in uncovering and highlighting the manifestations of human plight, joblessness, inequalities, malnutrition, hunger, diseases, and squalor that afflict the region's inhabitants of urban squatters settlements, slums, shanties, or rural villages. Unless these problems can be highlighted and confronted with national urgency, it will be virtually impossible to effectively target resources to improve the conditions of the poor.

STRENGTHENING INTERNATIONAL ASSISTANCE

How much the international community really contributes to support the goals of poverty reduction in Southern Africa is very much open to debate. There are many aid packages, both bilateral and multilateral in nature. The bilateral commitments are often difficult to assess because the details surrounding those efforts may only be known by the two countries concerned. The multilateral programs we are most familiar with, on the other hand—such as those funded by the World Bank, IMF, UN organizations, and other lending institutions—are much more accessible and open to public scrutiny. But some of their activities are also shrouded in the extensive conditionality attached to them. That is, some of them dispense aid to do what they want to accomplish instead of supporting the recipient countries' national priorities.

For example, economic aid from the World Bank and IMF under SAPs has always come with strings attached. Their stringent conditions have required, *inter alia*, state interventions in the economy to be minimized, the privatization of public enterprises, and economic management left largely to market incentives. The experience has been disastrous in country after country in the region, from Zambia to Zimbabwe, Malawi, and Mozambique where SAPs were applied. Here, unemployment has soared and poverty levels have escalated. In villages and cities, the World Bank and IMF "cure" has instead imposed severe social costs and hardships on the people, hurting the very vulnerable groups that most needed relief. Households have suffered hard times to the point of being compelled to eat only two meals a day, leading to severe malnourishment, hunger, disease, and stunted growth for children. Large numbers of children have also dropped out of school for want of school fees, resulting further in plummeting school enrollments.[9]

Opportunities, however, lie in utilizing resources of other UN agencies to the maximum benefit. Agencies like ILO, FAO, WHO, and others maintain strong field operations capable of providing direct economic and technical assistance to the poor, and their assistance is virtually without any adverse conditions. Those organizations have clearly defined agendas in their areas of competencies: ILO, in employment creation and labor working conditions within the interactive tripartite structures of government, business, and labor; FAO in the food security area; and WHO in disease control, immunization, and other health-related issues. Their contributions in these fields have remained unassailable.

Other UN programs and funds, including principally UNDP, UNICEF, and UNFPA, also possess tremendous potential and capacity to deliver assistance directly to the poor. Their ideals are much closer to the people than the loftier goals pursued by the World Bank and IMF. However, viewed from their field operational performance, these organizations have performed below par, largely because they do not appear to be mission-driven and therefore lack a coherent focus. They instead haphazardly tackle issues from poverty to HIV/AIDS, job creation, domestic violence, and so on without achieving any real impact in any of them. Their efforts have often been marred by their own huge bureaucratic demands and preoccupations that place greater emphasis on procedure and form (preparing studies and plans after plans, and engaging in endless consultations with governments or NGOs) rather than substance (providing real deliverables in goods and services directly to the needy). They have tended to spend inordinately long periods on consultations and developing or perfecting their modes of intervention instead of actual delivery. Meanwhile, poverty has continued to deepen, HIV/AIDS to spread, malnourished children to die, and pain and anguish to escalate throughout the societies they serve. Clearly, aid delayed is aid denied!

Two policy instruments are critical to strengthening aid coordination. First, at the country and regional levels, there should be locally developed plans for poverty reduction through which international assistance should be programmed and coordinated. That should be a fundamental national requirement. Even aid donors should not advance funding in the absence of clearly articulated national priorities and objectives within a plan framework. All external assistance should be required to fulfill locally determined priorities in combating poverty and promoting development objectives and needs without imposing excessive conditions. This would facilitate a swift and more efficient delivery of external aid, while, at the same time, reducing the chances of official corruption or fraud, for example, a government minister would divert donor funds from a rural road-building project to personal use. Second, countries themselves need to shift their priorities. More and more state resources should be devoted to poverty reduction or poverty-impact programs than emphasizing major highway and airport improvement projects. Poverty-impact priorities should always include the expansion of employment opportunities, provision of basic and adult education, primary health care, clean water supply and adequate sanitation, nutrition, and the creation of social safety nets for the most vulnerable in the society. This thrust of prioritization in conjunction with the "mainstreaming" of poverty programs in national budgets would go a long way toward stemming the tide in the fight against poverty.

While there is merit for debt relief for the highly indebted poor countries (HIPC) such as Mozambique and Zambia, the exercise must include more effective resource programming as part of the external assistance for poverty reduction. Otherwise, any funds released from debt forgiveness could fall into a bottomless black hole, unaccounted for and without much impact on poverty-reduction efforts whatsoever. I propose that HIPC programs require plans to be drawn up by the indebted countries, demonstrating clearly the intended utilization of HIPC dividends—the funds released from debt servicing—for poverty-reduction purposes, including expansion of education and health-care services as well as creating employment opportunities for the poor. Without such plans, debt relief would be an endless exercise in futility that would always finance military armament, official corruption, or excessive travels abroad by the high-ranking ruling elites—déjà vu all over again.

Conclusion

Absolute poverty in this region is a truly daunting challenge. But it can be tackled through a combination of vision, political will, and tangible, proactive policy strategies and programs. The overemphasis on the need for resources, meaning "money," to deal with poverty is largely misplaced. What is required is the political commitment as well as organizational structures to address these human ills.

There exist, in Southern Africa, extremely disturbing contradictions. There are poor peasants and rich industrialists living side by side; those with skills and opportunities, jobs, incomes, land, and wealth cohabiting with the vast majority without any; those who "count" politically, economically, and socially coexisting with those who do not. Obviously, this is a prescription for disaster. It is a threat to peace and regional stability. Therefore, fighting poverty is in the region's self-interest. Like the fight against colonialism and apartheid in South Africa and Namibia, the struggle against poverty and for social justice is equally a fight for freedom. The alternative of continued human suffering, anguish, and misery could only precipitate another endless cycle of violence, crime, civil conflict, and social turmoil that would retard the regional development.

Fundamentally, conflicts in the region have been waged over political power and resources. Now that political power is in indigenous hands, it is imperative to tackle the issues of equitable distribution of wealth and resources, including land. Governments alone cannot accomplish this enormous task, nor can it be tackled successfully by the civil society sector acting independently. It requires broad-based partnerships of governments, community groups, NGOs, business, peasant farmers, and grassroots advocacy organizations. But governments must lead! Real change and development can come about only through the people, facilitated by an enabling politico-social environment. Thus, governments must fulfill a set of critical elements to promote development in the region, including commitment to peace and peaceful resolution of conflicts; forging democratic institutions that enhance popular participation; promoting economic growth with social justice; enhancing opportunities and social empowerment to achieve sustainable livelihood for all; ensuring transparency and accountability in governance, including wiping out the scourge of official corruption; and respecting the rule of law and basic human rights.

These are musts. There is too much at stake at the moment. Today's regional leaders cannot afford to fail their people in these critical areas of need. If they do, tomorrow's younger generations must rightly condemn them for bequeathing a defiled human habitat.

NOTES

PROLOGUE

1. The suspended group comprised myself and old friends and comrades Gilson Kaweche, Gideon Ndhlovu, Gibson Zimba, Moses Mumbi (mhsrp), Zayeko Zimba (mhsrp), Potpher Kabandami, and William Kayamba (mhsrp). Five of us were reinstated at Chizongwe following intervention by then minister of education John Mwanakatwe and his deputy, Henry Thorncroft, while Zakeyo Zimba, Kabandami, and Kayamba were transferred to Munali in Lusaka to complete their form V.

INTRODUCTION

1. Representatives from twelve SADC countries attended the two regional poverty forums in Namibia (May 1997) and South Africa (November 1997) but, due to the timing of their admission into SADC, both the Democratic Republic of the Congo (DRC) and Seychelles did not participate.

2. "Poverty in the democratic era demands a critical media mirror." *The Sunday Independent,* April 13, 1997.

CHAPTER ONE

1. "Introduction" to *Southern Africa: Toward Economic Liberation.* Amon J. Nsekela ed. (London: Rex Collings, 1981), pp. vii–viii. President Khama was at the time referring to only nine member countries of the original SADCC, namely Angola, Botswana, Lesotho, Malawi, Mozambique, Swaziland, Tanzania, Zambia, and Zimbabwe.

2. Greg Lanning and Marti Mueller, *Africa Undermined: Mining Companies and the Underdevelopment of Africa.* (Harmondsworth: Penguin, 1979), pp. 485–488.

3. Ibid., pp. 485–486.

4. Ibid., p. 70.

5. C. S. L. Chachage, Magnus Ericsson and Peter Gibbon, *Mining and Structural Adjustment: Studies on Zimbabwe and Tanzania.* (Uppsala: Nordiska Afrikainstitutet, 1993), pp. 14–16; and Lanning and Mueller, pp. 73–77.

6. See, for example, "Mozambican Studies: Underdevelopment and Migrant Labour" *Journal of Social Science.* Vol. 1, No. 1, 1980.

7. Karl Max, *Capital.* (London: Allen and Urwin, 1940, reprint), p. 59.

8. Lanning and Mueller, p. 496.

9. For excellent surveys, see Phyllis Johnson and David Martin eds., *Destructive Engagement: Southern Africa at War.* (Harare: Zimbabwe Publishing House, 1986), and *Apartheid Terrorism:*

The Destabilization Report. (London: The Commonwealth Secretariat, James Currey, 1989).

10. Richard Cornwell, "Democratization and Security in Africa" *African Security Review.* Vol. 16, No. 5, 1997, pp. 16–18.

11. Of course, recorded accounts of anti-colonial resistance by various indigenous societies of the region date back as far as the beginning of the European incursions in Africa and genesis of colonialism some three to four hundred years ago, especially in Angola, Mozambique, and South Africa. See accounts by Colin Legum, *The Battlefronts of Southern Africa.* (New York: Africana Publishing Co., 1988).

12. See Marga Holness "Angola: The Struggle Continues" in Johnson and Martin eds. *Destructive Engagement,* pp. 73–109; and Eduardo Mondlane, *The Struggle for Mozambique.* (Harmondsworth: Penguin, 1969).

13. See Legum, *The Battlefronts,* pp. 22–42.

14. Extensively covered by R. Davies, D. O'Meara, and S. Dlamini, *The Struggle for South Africa—A Reference Guide to Movements, Organizations and Institutions.* Vol. 2 (London: Zed Books, 1985); and Brian Wood ed. *Namibia 1884–1984: Readings on Namibia's History and Society.* (London: Namibia Support Committee and UN Institute for Namibia, 1985).

15. See Jurgen Schadeberg ed. *Nelson Mandela and the Rise of the ANC from the Pages of Drum Magazine.* (London: Bloomsburg, 1990) "Foreword" by Walter Sisulu.

16. Keith Gottschalk, "The South African State in Namibia: From Colonialism to Counter-Revolution" in Wood ed. *Namibia 1884–1984,* p. 496.

17. See United Nations, *Namibia: The Trust Betrayed.* (New York: UN, 1969).

18. See Legum, *The Battlefronts,* pp. 104–124; Johnson and Martin, *Destructive Engagement,* Chapters 8 and 9; and *Apartheid Terrorism,* pp. 3–9.

19. See Christopher Pycroft, Barry Munslow, with Mark Adams, *Southern Africa Annual Review 1987/1988.* Vol. 2. (London: Hans Zell Publishers, 1990), pp. 147–148; and pp. 148–149.

20. See Gillian and Susan Cronje, *The Workers of Namibia.* (London: International Defence and Aid Fund, 1979).

21. See Nsekela, *Southern Africa,* pp. 214–218; and Johnson and Martin, *Destructive Engagement,* pp.139–169.

22. See SADCC 2: *Transport and Communications Projects.* (Gaborone: SADCC Annual Reports, 1981 and 1983); and mimeographed tables for 1981 and 1983 projects; also Johnson and Martin, *Apartheid Terrorism,* pp. 52–59 and 90–95.

23. SADCC, *Policy and Strategy for Food, Agriculture and Natural Resources.* (Gaborone: SADCC, 987); and Second Carnegie Conference Papers, *Proceedings of the Second Carnegie Enquiry into Poverty and Development in Southern Africa.* (Cape Town: University of Cape Town, 1984).

24. Martin Plaut, Elaine Unterhalter, and David Ward, *The Struggle for Southern Africa.* (London: War and Want Liberation, 1981), p. 29; and *South,* November 1981.

25. See UN/ECA, *The Effects on Botswana, Lesotho, Swaziland and Mozambique of Sanctions Imposed Against South Africa.* A/CONF.107/1 (Paris, March 1981).

26. Plaut, Unterhalter, and Ward, *The Struggle for Southern Africa,* p. 30.

27. See UNICEF report, *Children on the Frontline* (New York: UNICEF, 1989, third edition), p. 14; and Pycroft and Munslow, with Adams, *Southern Africa,* p. 300.

28. Pycroft and Munslow, with Adams, *Southern Africa*, p. 300.

29. See a survey of the African situation in Bade Onimode, ed. *The IMF, The World Bank and The African Debt: The Social and Political Impact.* Vol. 2. (London: Zed books, 1989).

30. World Bank, *Trends in Developing Economies 1990.* (Washington D.C.: World Bank, 1990), p. 613.

31. Ibid., pp. 61, 315, 327, 376, and 622.

32. Yukon Huang and Peter Nicholas, "The Social Costs of Adjustment" *Finance and Development,* June 1987, pp. 22–24; Peter Heller, "Fund-Supported Adjustment Programs and the Poor" *Finance and Development,* December 1988, pp. 2–5; "Analyzing the Effects of Structural Adjustment" *The Courier*, No. 116 (July–August 1989), pp. 12–15; and World Bank, *Making Adjustment Work for the Poor.* (Washington D.C.: World Bank, 1990).

33. E. V. K. Jaycox, *Africa: From Stagnation to Reform.* (Washington D.C.: World Bank, February 1993).

34. Donatella Lorch, "In Zambia a Legacy of Graft and Drug Scandal Taint Democratic Reforms" *New York Times,* Sunday, January 30, 1994, p. 10.

35. UNDP, *Human Development Report 1997.* (New York: Oxford Univ. Press), p. 101.

CHAPTER TWO

1. Robert S. McNamara, *The McNamara Years at the World Bank: Major Policy Addresses of Robert S. McNamara 1968–81.* (Baltimore: World Bank, 1981).

2. Potentially, South Africa could rival Mauritius, but its figures represent a distorted picture as a result of the apartheid history of racially biased statistics.

   Therefore, various sources were used with respect to South Africa, for example, Reconstruction and Development Programme (RDP) *Key Indicators of Poverty in South Africa.* (RDP Office, 1995) and the report by Julius May et al., *Poverty and Inequality in South Africa,* 13 May 1998. (Durban: Praxis Publishing, 1998).

3. See conference papers and reports from the "Regional Forum on Poverty Eradication in Southern Africa". Phase I, Windhoek, Namibia 13–15 May 1997; and Phase II, Midrand, South Africa 3–6 November 1997.

4. Graca Machel, *Report on the Impact of Armed Conflict on Children.* (New York: UNICEF, 1996); and UNICEF, *Children on the Frontlines, op. cit.*

5. Analysis draws on background presentations and reports of the "Regional Forums on Poverty," Phases I and II (1997).

CHAPTER THREE

1. See Pycroft and Munslow, with Adams, *Southern Africa,* Chapters 19–21.

2. Hussein Solomon and Jakkie Cilliérs, eds. *People, Poverty and Peace*, IDP No. 4 May 1996. (Johannesburg: Halfway House, 1996), pp. 4–13.

3. See "NGOs Declare War on Poverty" *NGO Matters,* Special Edition Vol. 2. No. 9 August 1997; and Julian May et al. *Poverty and Inequality in South Africa, op. cit.*

4. The Ceasefire Campaign Report, "The Struggle for the Soul of the Southern African Development Community—Development or Militarization?" National Conference, Johannesburg, South Africa 16–17 April 1999.

CHAPTER FOUR

1. South African statistics, however, are highly distorted and do not measure much progress. They are highly suspect in view of their strong racial biases as a legacy of apartheid.

2. See for instance, Kjell J. Havnevik, *Tanzania: The Limits to Development from Above.* (Uppsala: Nordiska Afrikainstitutet, 1993).

3. Idriss Jazairy et al. *The State of World Rural Poverty.* (New York: IFAD, New York University Press, 1992), pp. 29–30.

4. Quoted in *NGO Matters*, p. 7.

CHAPTER FIVE

1. Havnevik, *Tanzania: The Limits to Development from Above, op. cit.*

2. Material in this section is drawn heavily from conference papers presented at the "UN Regional Forum on Poverty Eradication in Southern Africa," Phases I and II held in Windhoek, Namibia 13–15 May 1997; and Midrand, South Africa 3–6 November

1997. Hereafter to be cited only as "Namibian Poverty Forum, Phase I," (1997) and "South African Poverty Forum, Phase II," (1997), respectively.

3. Background paper on "The Angolan Experience" by Maria Umba, Domingas Goncalo, Julio Mendonca, and Mateus Muanda; and "A Poverty Reduction Strategy for Mozambique" by Maimuna Assiate Ibraimo, presented to the "Namibian Poverty Forum, Phase I" (1997) and "South African Poverty Forum, Phase II," (1997), respectively.

4. Ibraimo, "A Poverty Reduction Strategy for Mozambique."

5. Background paper on "Efforts Being Undertaken in Botswana to Address Poverty and Unemployment Problems" by G. Moatshe, A. Tamuhla, and Morris Nyathi, presented at the "Namibian Poverty Forum, Phase I," (1997).

6. Ibid.

7. Background paper on "Lesotho's Experience in Dealing with Anti-Poverty Issues: Government and Non-Governmental Initiatives," presented by J. Majalle, M. Mokhothu, M. Tsehlo, and L. Keketso to the "South African Poverty Forum, Phase II," (1997).

8. Quoted in Ibid.

9. Ibid.

10. Excellent presentation in background papers on "Conditions of Poverty, Unemployment and Social Disintegration and Steps Taken: Case of Malawi" by Lingalireni Mihowa, David Faiti, Misheck Longwe, Felix Mponda, and Janet Karim, and "Uplifting of Women's Economic and Social Status: Towards Sustainable Socio-economic Development and Poverty Alleviation in Malawi"

by Janet Karim to the "Namibian Poverty Forum, Phase I," (1997).

11. "Conditions of Poverty, Unemployment. Case of Malawi," by Mihowa et al. p. 2.

12. See "Background papers on NGO Involvement in Poverty Eradication in Namibia" by NANGOF, and "Background Paper on Namibia's Efforts in Poverty Alleviation" by The Namibian Economic Policy Research Unit, to the "Namibian Poverty Forum, Phase I," (1997).

13. Namibia's statistics like those of South Africa as presented in Table 5.1 relating to per capita GNP, life expectancy, illiteracy, human development, etc. are still very much distorted because of their strong racial bias weighted in favor of the white minority population.

14. GINI coefficient—the measure of income inequality in society— is as high as 0.67 for Namibia compared with 0.61 for South Africa and 0.62 for Brazil.

15. Signatories to the declaration included the South African government, the South Africa Council of Churches, the South African NGO Coalition, the Homeless People's Federation, the UNDP, and the COSATU.

16. *Constitution of the Republic of South Africa.* Chapter 2, Bill of Rights, Sections 26–29.

17. "A man is left to die because he is too poor to live," *Sunday Times* (South Africa) November 30, 1997, p. 21.

18. See extensive presentations by South African participants, "Worcester Rural Area in Boland, Western Cape" by K. Kariem, "Country Experiences—Rural Areas, North-West Province" by

Kgakgamatso Lesie, Jane Mashigo, Judith Stungua, and Rev. H. Mononyane; "Northern Province" by Aldrin Ndalani, Paul Phuravhathu, David Khosa et al.; "Burgersdorp Young Women Educaton Group—Northern Province" by Shilivana, Gavaza, Mhanghweni, Bonn, Mafarana, and Sidan; and "Yinhle Lenfto YoungWomen'sClub—Mpumalanga"byMganduzweni,Jerusalem, Swalala, Mahushu, Mafifty, Kanyamazane, and Chochocho, to the "South African Poverty Forum, Phase II," (1997).

19. Office of the President, *Reconstruction and Development Programme*, 1995; and Julian May et al. *Poverty and Inequality in South Africa, op. cit.*

20. Office of the President, *Key Indicators of Poverty in South Africa, op. cit.*

21. Ibid.

22. UNDP, *Human Development Report 1997.* (New York: Oxford University Press, 1967) Table 1, pp. 146–148. Although its HDI of 0.716 placed South Africa in medium-income category, its data have serious racial biases and therefore distort the development picture.

23. See background paper on "Poverty in Swaziland and Special Problems Affecting Rural Women" by Zandile Tshabalala, "Poverty Alleviation—Swaziland" by Themba Dlamini; "Poverty Eradication—Swaziland" by Lavumisa Dlamini, and "Swaziland Experience in Dealing with Poverty, Unemployment and Social Disintegration and Special Problems Affecting Women" by Emmanual Mdlanyundi to the "South African Poverty Forum, Phase II," (1997).

24. Havnevik, *Tanzania: The Limits to Development from Above, op. cit.*

25. Background paper on "Tanzania's Experiences in Poverty Eradication" by Iziraiah Mukaruka, Chrispin Mdimi, and Jererali

Ulimwengu, presented to the "South African Poverty Forum, Phase II," (1997).

26. Ibid.

27. See an excellent and detailed background paper "Summary Analysis on Zambia," presented by Mulima Kufekisa Akapelwa, Eniwet Kakawa, John J. Musukuma, Samuel Ngoma, and Matondo Monde Yeta presented to the "Namibian Poverty Forum, Phase I," (1997).

28. Ibid.

29. Such a plan is understood to be in the works under the auspices of UNDP.

30. See "Summary Analysis on Zambia" paper presented by Mulima Kufekisa Akapelwa, Eniwet Kakawa, John J. Musukuma et al. to the "Namibian Poverty Forum, Phase I," (1997).

31. Sam Moyo has made extensive analyses of the land issues, see his *Economic Nationalism and Land Reform in Zimbabwe.* (Harare: Southern African Printing and Publishing House, 1995); and his paper on "Land Entitlements and Growing poverty in Southern Africa" presented to the "South African Poverty Forum, Phase II," (1997).

32. Out of the ninety-nine countries recently studied by Transparency International, Zimbabwe is the 48th most corrupt nation on the corruption perception index. The index measures perception of group and official fraud within countries whereby 1 represents the least corrupt (Sweden) and 99 the most corrupt (Cameroon). Measured against other countries of the region, Zimbabwe is the third most corrupt country after Tanzania (93) and Zambia (57).

CHAPTER SIX

1. The World Bank, *Countries: Botswana.* (Washington D.C., September 1999).

2. Robert L. Carry Jr. "Poverty and Mass Unemployment in Mineral-rich Botswana" *American Journal of Economics and Sociology.* 46(9) January 1987, pp. 71–87.

3. The World Bank, *The East Asian Miracle.* (New York: Oxford Univ. Press, 1993).

4. COSATU and SANGOCO were critical of GEAR as not having gone far enough in creating employment opportunities and guaranteeing social justice the way RDP had attempted to do.

5. The World Bank, *Reducing Poverty in South Africa,* pp. 53–54.

6. UNDP, *Overcoming Human Poverty.* (New York: UNDP, 1998), p. 37.

7. Ibid.

8. Commonwealth Secretariat, *Practical Mechanisms for Poverty Reduction.* (Manchester: University of Manchester, 1996), pp. 8–9.

9. See extensive treatments of issues by UNECA, *African Alternatives: Framework to Structural Adjustment Programs for Socio-Economic Recovery and Transformation.* (Addis Ababa: April 1991); A. M. Mwanza, ed. *The Structural Adjustment Programme in Zambia: Lessons from Experience.* (Harare: SAPES Books, 1992); and P. Gibbons, ed. *Structural Adjustment and Working Poor in Zimbabwe.* (Uppsala: Nordiska Afrikainstitutet, 1995).

SELECTED REFERENCES

Bryant, Coralie, ed. *Poverty, Policy and Food Security in Southern Africa*. Boulder, CO: Lynne Reinner Publications, 1988.

Conference papers of the "UN Regional Forum on Poverty Eradication in Southern Africa" Phase I, Windhoek, Namibia 13–15 May 1997; and Phase II, Midrand, South Africa 3–6 November 1997. (Over thirty country papers were presented on various themes of poverty.)

Davies, R., O'Meara, D., and Dlamini, S. *The Struggle for South Africa. A Reference Guide to Movements, Organizations and Institutions*. Vol. 2. London: Zed Books, 1985.

Gibbon, P. *Structural Adjustment and the Working Poor in Zimbabwe: Study of Labour, Women, Informal Sector Workers and Health*. Uppsala, Nordiska Afrikainstitutet, 1995.

Havnevik, Kjell J. *Tanzania: the Limits to Development from Above*. Uppsala: Nordiska Afrikainistitutet, 1993.

Johnson, Phyllis, and Martin, David, eds. *Destructive Engagement: Southern Africa at War*. Harare: Zimbabwe Publishing House, 1986.

_____. *Apartheid Terrorism: The Destabilization Report*. London: The Commonwealth Secretariat in Association with James Currer, 1989.

Jazairy, Idriss, et al. *The State of World Rural Poverty*. New York: IFAD, New York University Press, 1992.

Kowet, D. K. *Land, Labour Migration and Politics in Southern Africa: Botswana, Lesotho and Swaziland*. New York: Africana Publications, 1979.

Lanning, Greg with Mueller, Marti. *Africa Undermined: Mining Companies and the Underdevelopment of Africa*. Harmondsworth: Penguin, 1979.

Legum, Colin. *The Battlefronts of Southern Africa*. New York: Africana Publishing Company, 1988.

May, Julian, et al. *Poverty and Inequality in South Africa*. Durban: Praxis Publishing, 1998.

Mondlane, Eduardo. *The Struggle for Mozambique*. Harmondsworth: Penguin, 1969.

Moyo, Sam, et al. T*he Southern African Environment: Profiles of SADC Countries*. London: Earthscan Publications, 1993.

_____. *Economic Nationalism and Land Reform in Zimbabwe*. Harare: Southern Africa Printing and Publishing House, 1995.

Nsekela Amon J. *Southern Africa: Toward Economic Liberation*. London: Rex Collins, 1981.

Report of the Second Carnegie Inquiry into Poverty and Development in Southern Africa. Cape Town, South Africa, 1984. (311 papers on various themes of poverty and development.)

Smith, Susanna. *Frontline Africa: The Right to a Future: An Oxfam Report on Conflict and Poverty in Southern Africa*. London: Oxfam, 1990.

UNDP. *Zambia: Human Development Report 1997*. Lusaka: UNDP, 1997.

_____. *Human Development Report 1997*. New York: Oxford University Press, 1997.

_____. *Overcoming Human Poverty*. New York: UNDP, 1998.

UNICEF. *Children and Women in South Africa. A Situation Analysis*. Johannesburg: UNICEF, 1993.

_____. *Malawi: Situation Analysis of Poverty*. Lilongwe: UNICEF, 1993.

_____. *Children and Women in Zimbabwe*. Harare: UNICEF, 1994.

Wood, Brian, ed. *Namibia 1884–1984: Readings on Namibia's History and Society*. London: Namibia Support Committee and UN Institute for Namibia, 1985.

World Bank. *Malawi: Human Resources and Poverty: Profile and Priorities for Action*. Washington D.C.: World Bank, 1996.

_____. *Zambia: Poverty Assessment.*
Washington D.C.: World Bank, 1996.

_____. *Tanzania: The Challenge of Reforms: Growth, Incomes and Welfare.* Washington D.C.: World Bank, 1996.

_____. *Poverty Reduction and the World Bank: Progress and Challenges in the 1990s.* Washington D.C.: World Bank, 1996.

INDEX

severe poverty and human development crisis in, 98–99

Malnutrition, 27, 28, 29, 32, 34, 38, 49, 51, 59, 61, 68, 80, 111, 116, 128

Mandela, Nelson, 25, 47, 69, 121, 135

Maputo, 28

Masire, Ketumile, 121

Masvingo, severe poverty in Katule village of, 28

Mauritius, 27, 44, 60, 64, 76–77, 90, 92, 104;
HDI and GDI rankings for, 64, 76–77, 90, 92, 104

Mbeki, Thabo, xix

McNamara, Robert, 59

Midrand, xvii, xviii, 26

Migrant labor, 28, 41, 69, 98

Movement for Multiparty Democracy (MMD), 2;
and offshoot parties of, 11, 12

Mozambique, 27, 28, 33, 38, 43, 44, 45, 46, 47, 48, 49, 50, 51, 52, 61, 63, 64, 67, 68, 69, 71, 77, 79, 80, 81, 86, 87, 88, 90, 91, 92–94, 107, 110, 120, 129, 131;
debt by, 52;
HDI and GDI rankings for, 64, 77, 90, 92;
the 1992 peace accord of, 91, 93;

Mozambique National Resistance (RENAMO), 68

Muluzi, Bakili, 99

Mwanawasa, Levy, 9, 16

Namibia, 7, 18, 26, 28, 29, 30, 31, 38, 39, 40, 43, 44, 45, 46, 47, 50, 51, 54, 60, 61, 63, 64, 67, 70, 73, 77, 79, 85, 86, 87, 88, 89, 90, 92, 100–101, 102, 120, 122, 123, 124, 132;
HDI and GDI rankings for, 64, 77, 90, 92;
poverty and development challenges in, 100–101

National budgets, linking poverty to, 119, 127–28

National Citizen Coalition (NCC), 9

National Front for the Liberation of Angola (FNLA), 44

National Leadership for Development (NLD), xxiv, 9

National Union for the Total Independence of Angola (UNITA), 44

Nchelenge district, 28

Ndola, 14

New Xade, squalid conditions for the San people of, 28

Northern Cape Province, squalor among the Mier community of, 28

Nyerere, Julius, 108

Ongulumbatshe, 45

Opposition members of parliament, appointment of, 21

Ovitoto, 28

Parliament, 16, 20, 21, 30, 78, 106, 113, 126;
and Speaker of, 78

Patriotic Front (PF), 9

Peace, 25, 26, 27, 29, 31, 33, 34, 56, 67, 68–69, 70, 71, 72, 88, 91, 93, 102, 105, 117, 118, 119, 120, 121, 122, 132;
new paradigms of, 68;
peace and development, viii, 120

Policy determinants, 85

Popular Movement for the Liberation of Angola (MPLA), 44

Portuguese colonialism, 44

Poverty, as number one enemy, 29;
definition and dimensions of, 59, 60;
feminization of, 112;
hearings on, xviii;
reduction agenda of, 88, 119;

152

social indicators of, 92;
spatial concentrations (in South Africa) of, 104;
UN regional forums on, 26, 73, 120

Ramphal, Sir Shridal, 30
Rand Monetary Area, 50
Reconstruction and Development Programme (RDP), 105
Refugee burden, 33, 38, 50–56
Reindustrialization, 14
Rhodes, John Cecil, and mining ventures by, 40
Rhodesia, 45, 46;
fight against nationalist movements by, 46
Rural women, 13, 34, 38, 61, 70, 73, 74, 78–80, 81, 82, 83, 85, 86, 96

SADC Parliamentary Forum, 20
Shared growth, 122, 123, 124
Social Democratic Party (SDP), 9
Social infrastructure and the rebuilding of, 7, 15, 24, 43, 88, 93, 94, 98
Southern Africa, definition of, 27–28;
colonial investment patterns and policies in, 38–43;
poorest countries in, 27, 56;
social poverty indicators for, 92
Southern African Development Community (SADC), 27
Southern African Development Coordination Conference (SADCC), 37
South Africa, 8, 14, 18, 25, 26, 28, 29, 30, 31, 38, 39, 40, 41, 42, 43, 44, 45, 46, 47, 48, 49, 50, 51, 52, 56, 60, 61, 63, 64, 67, 68, 69, 70, 71, 73, 76, 77, 78, 79, 80, 81, 85, 86, 87, 88, 89, 90, 91, 92, 94, 97, 101, 102-6, 114, 120, 121, 122, 123, 124, 128, 132;

colonial development experiences of, 42-43;
extreme wealth amid abject poverty in, 102;
HDI and GDI rankings for, 64, 76, 77, 90, 92, 104
South African Council of Churches, 47
South African Customs Union (SACU), 50
South West Africa People's Organization (SWAPO), 7, 44
Statism, 55, 87, 99
Structural adjustment programs (SAPs), 52, 79
Sustainable development, 48, 62, 117, 119, 126
Swaziland, 44, 46, 48, 49, 51, 64, 68, 77, 80, 86, 90, 92, 105, 106-7;
HDI and GDI rankings for, 64, 77, 90, 92;
impact of HIV/AIDS in, 107;
status of women in, 107;
traditions and development challenges in, 107

Tanzania, 27, 44, 51, 54, 64, 67, 77, 78, 80, 86, 88, 89, 90, 92, 107, 108;
HDI and GDI rankings for, 64, 77, 90, 92;
poverty and socialist transformation challenges in, 107-9;
Transkei, 28, 49, 70, 104
Truman. Harry S., 24
Truth and Reconciliation Commission, xix

Ubuntu, xviii
Ujamaa vijijini, 108
Underdevelopment, 38, 90, 110
Unemployment, 1, 3, 8, 14, 27, 28, 29, 32, 34, 51, 52, 53, 54, 60, 63, 69,